Dedication

For MM

I hope this is
a blessing to you.

Sarah.

nyesarah@yahoo.co.uk.

Whose Child?

UK Abortion and the Gospel Message

Foreword

I have known S. Nye for a number of years. Also I have worked with her and observed her compassionate heart and her analytical mind. I feel honoured to give this foreword to this impressive, and much needed book.

S. Nye has poured out her heart and her head into the writing of this most valuable book. I doubt if there is another as informative about the truth of abortion and as supportive of the women who have already had abortions. These women are now suffering the effects of the brutal ending of life of the child within. But there is no support from the Abortion Clinics.

S. Nye's heart is for the unborn child whose life is considered of no value, her heart is also for the women who have been forced to have an abortion through pressure from family, career or finances. This book is also an expression of her head, her analytical mind, which demands the truth, the evidence of accurate scientific research. She has meticulously given her every research reference on each page. Therefore it is easy for the reader to check on the facts that she has written.

"Who's Child" is definitely not designed to bring condemnation on women who have had abortions but to help them overcome the terrible side effects. It also would help women considering abortion if they were told exactly what they are about to do to the unborn child in their womb. The massive scale of abortion surely makes it the number one social justice issue of our time.

I highly recommend that you read this book so that you are equipped to play your part in prayer and action on behalf of the unborn.

Hilary Walker,
Assistant Pastor of Oxford Bible Church.

Preface

The subject of this book is far too close to home for many, and for others it has become a taboo subject. It is one of the most contentious moral issues of our day, involving such heart-breaking situations that there seems to be no hope of adequate solutions.

And yet, if we can take a challenging look at the arguments put forward to justify abortion, this will inevitably cause us to take a fresh look at what it means to be human. There is good news to be shared.

Included in the book are two chapters on forgiveness and I hope that no one can see this book as in any way condemnatory. This is one of the church's main fears yet this should not deter us from broaching such a vital subject.

"Whose Child?" is broad in its subject-matter since it is just a brief introduction to some vital issues which are each worthy of a book to themselves. We start at the foundational level of defining what it is that makes us human in the first place, then at what point in life that humanity begins. Building up from there, we consider whether abortion is or is not a legitimate and necessary solution to the very real needs we see in society today. We reflect on what we individually, and as churches, can do to be a part of the solution.

Chapters discussing the arguments used to justify abortion are followed by an overview of the damage done to women spiritually, emotionally and physically. Building from there, we go on to the damage to the nation of abortion, with Biblical Israel as our model. We look at what the Bible teaches and whether biology confirms biblical thinking. We discuss if and under what circumstances abortion might be ethically justifiable, and consider the spiritual ramifications in the church and the nation of abortion's acceptance as a common practice.

The ideas of the book build upon each other so that the most important conclusions are in the final few chapters. The aim is to demonstrate that this is a subject of the utmost importance and that the church is in need of repentance. At the end of the book there are practical signposts to help people affected by abortion to get the help they need and to help others. To that aim, there is an interview with David Brennan, head of Brephos.org, a ministry which assists churches to respond to abortion from the pulpit. This section also gives information about organisations which can help people who are contemplating abortion or women suffering from negative effects from it.

I aim to be relatively unemotional in my approach. Where it is possible, factual information is derived from neutral, or pro-abortion sources. As believers, we believe what the Bible tells us, but we also see that biology and experience support and confirm what the Bible teaches. We will see that reasons for the protection of the unborn are entirely logical and rational.

In order to fully understand the extent and wonder of the good news of the Gospel on this subject, we must understand the extent of the bad news. This book may be a difficult read especially for those who have had some involvement with abortion. For this reason I have placed part of the "Good News" chapter on the forgiveness of God at the beginning.

This is mainly aimed at the biblical Christian church in Britain and the Bible is quoted as the final authority. But other sources also point independently to the destructive effects of abortion and confirm biblical truth. Christians are afraid of appearing unloving, but it is unloving to remain silent when we have the answer which the world needs. We can help people to choose life for their children and come alongside those who have had an abortion as they find forgiveness and full healing. It is my hope that this book helps in this process.

Notes:

1) For Bible references, unless otherwise stated, the New American Standard Version is quoted.

2) I am aware that "Satan" as a Proper Noun is spelt with an upper case "s" but I have chosen to use the lower case.

3) In the interests of using neutral language where possible, the unborn child, or "fetus" or "embryo" is referred to throughout the book simply as "the unborn." However, neutrality is not possible when using pronouns for the unborn: Since we know that the sex of any human being is determined at conception, the unborn cannot be referred to as "it" but must be referred to as "he or she".

We are destroying arguments and
all arrogance raised against the knowledge of God...
(2 Cor. 10.5)

Contents

Whose Child?

UK Abortion and the Gospel Message

Chapter 1A: Forgiveness

Since it is vital to understand the full implications of abortion in order to be able to do anything about it, most of this book will deal with the "bad news" of the damage which it causes. But even more importantly, we need to understand that however difficult the circumstances, this need not be the end of the story since God's grace is greater. There will be a discussion of the specific areas in which people can find forgiveness and healing with God in **chapter 1B, "Restoration"** (p.113). But firstly, in order not to be overwhelmed by the negatives, let's have an overview of the Good News, specifically on this subject. If you have had some involvement with abortion, what can be done?

We all have free choice, and although those choices may be heavily tinged by manipulation from outside influences, we need to take responsibility for all choices we have made. Only then is it possible to take back control of our existence, reject death and choose life. Satan, (the thief) comes to steal, kill and destroy, **(John 10.10)** which is what we choose once we have chosen abortion. But this need not be the end of the story; we still have the possibility to choose life.

It is something we must opt *into*. We have to choose to value what the Lord values, and want what He wants for us. We can choose the blessing or choose the curse, life with God or death apart from Him, forgiveness or judgement, not just for ourselves but for our families.[1] Fundamentally, God's response to those who have had an abortion is the same as His response to everyone, regardless of what kind of life they have led, since no human being can match up to His righteousness.[2]

But abortion brings the same sense of shame, guilt and fear as the Original Sin which caused Adam and Eve to hide from God. It is our natural reaction to hide in fear and keep this to ourselves. It is also a natural reaction to shut our eyes to the reality of what we have done and refuse to find out about the truth because of feelings of condemnation, or because we think there can be no solution to it. It takes courage to open our eyes and stop running away, but this is what is needed so that we can be made right with God and receive full healing.

Recognition of responsibility is required not just from the women who have had an abortion. Anyone who has been involved in it by **having, financing, performing, facilitating, encouraging** or **forcing** an abortion needs to be courageous and face this sin, calling it what it is and receiving God's complete forgiveness.[3]

---

[1] **Deuteronomy 30.19:** I call heaven and earth to witness against you today, that I have placed before you life and death, the blessing and the curse. So choose life in order that you may live, you and your descendants…

[2] **Romans 3.23:** …for all have sinned and fall short of the glory of God…

[3] **1 John 1.8-9:** If we say that we have no sin, we are deceiving ourselves and the truth is not in us. If we confess our sins, He is faithful and righteous

The fundamental message of the Cross is the Father's mercy, faithfulness and love, His commitment to mankind and His creation. That commitment extends to each one of us, and to the deepest part of us.

The vital subject of forgiveness continues later in the book in **chapter 1B, "Restoration,"** (p.113) but in order to understand this better we have to find out what we have been saved *from*. Finally, remember that however deep the sin, hurt and sense of condemnation may be, the well of God's love is deeper.

---

to forgive us our sins and to cleanse us from all unrighteousness.

Chapter 2: Who am I?

"Who am I?" is perhaps the most important question which any of us can ask, a question which preoccupies us often from adolescence onwards. The importance of this subject is made clear by the fact that it is also the source of changing western attitudes over the last few decades to sexuality, marriage, family, race and class. How we value ourselves and others dictates to a large extent what we may think about whether the unborn have value.

2a: Who does our Culture say I am?

A book could be written on this subject but broadly speaking our current progressive, western culture tells us that individuals have complete autonomy, every self-help book assuring us that we are able to choose our own destiny and that we can choose who and even what we are. Secular ideas harmonise with this, leading us to the inevitable conclusion that we are in fact free from the rules and regulations of repressive religion, so as a consequence we will be whoever and whatever we decide to be. In effect, we define ourselves.

This view of individual identity has been modelled in an increasingly overt way over the last fifty years, and could now be described as mainstream thinking, as represented in most major UK universities and media outlets.

But whether we like to admit it or not, this self-definition is heavily influenced by outside forces such as the following:

I am who you say I am

I have value according to my popularity with friends and on social media etc. So I have value if I am popular. By the same logic, if I am unpopular I will have no value. Increasing incidence of self-harm and suicide of teenagers following online (or other) bullying, demonstrates the widespread belief in this way of valuing human beings, (a widely-held belief at least among children and young adults). This is ultimately and sadly due to the acceptance of another person's opinion of us as being Truth.

I am who my boss says I am

I have more value the more materially productive I am. This is related to the idea that increased wealth increases a person's value. The obvious result of this thinking is to conclude that those who are not productive have no value, so the elderly and disabled who are not economically active, are hence not considered important. This is not usually overtly stated, but the increased acceptance over the last couple of decades of assisted suicide as being a reasonable solution for disabled people and those suffering from cognitive decline in old age, attests to the rising influence of this framework of thinking.

My life has no more or less value than that of an animal

The logical moral conclusion of evolutionism is that all living beings have an equal right to life, and that human beings are not special except that they have managed up until now to subdue other animal life. So if we can speak of a human having more "rights" than an animal, it is only the right that the more powerful and intelligent animal has over the less powerful.

I am who my parents say I am

Most of us fight against this definition from our first teenaged years. But the increasingly widespread practice of abortion tells me clearly that ultimately I only have value according to whether I am loved and wanted by my parents.

These are just some of the many influences which can affect our thinking and form the premise upon which we value ourselves. Since individuals define themselves, that identity is rooted only in the person's own shifting emotions and thoughts. Those emotions are fed by education, media influence, life experience and many other variables. Ultimately, humans have no fixed identity according to this framework of thinking.

2b: Who does the Bible say that I am?

The Bible tells us that we are made in the image of God.[4] This deceptively simple concept is the foundational Biblical teaching upon which relies every later teaching, not least that of Salvation. This means that our identity and the specialness of human life rely on this knowledge alone. Christians have pondered the ways in which we are made in God's image. We reflect His triune nature by possession of an intellect, emotions and will. We have the capacity to be self-aware, just as our Creator is self-aware rather than being a "force" or thing. We share with Him the capacity to consider the morality of our actions, we are relational in nature just as He is, and we are capable of having a relationship with Him.

Added to this is the concept of vice-regency: we were made in the image of a God who looks after and protects us in order for us to look after and protect those entrusted to our care. The Bible teaches that *all* human beings have supreme value because of the existence of God, and because of the value *He* places on us, regardless of our level of development, any disability, race, sex or perceived imperfection. Dr John Wyatt[5] writes, "In Christian thought, the dignity of a human being resides, not in what you can do, but in what you are, by creation. Human beings do not need to earn the right to be treated as Godlike beings. Our dignity is intrinsic, in the way we have been made".[6] So regardless of a person's level of development, or their

---

[4] **Genesis 1.27:** God created man in His own image, in the image of God He created him; male and female He created them.
[5] Professor of Ethics and Perinatology at University College London (UCL)

intellectual or physical capacity, to destroy *any* human being is an attack on His image. And to destroy that image in another is also to destroy His image in ourselves, since one of our functions is to protect and nurture.

The first murder recorded in the scriptures is Cain's murder of Abel. God's response is to place a curse on the murderer.[7] This curse demonstrates the importance God places on the matter of killing an innocent person.

Later we see the reason for this importance. After Noah's flood, God makes a new covenant with man, instituting the death penalty for murder. The explicit reason for such a severe penalty is because it is an attack on God's image.[8]

Thus the true meaning of the rainbow, rather than concerning our own often-changing perception of who we are, is based on our God-given identity as image-bearers of God.

---

[6] Wyatt, J, *Matters of Life and Death,* IVP/CMF, 2012, page 61
[7] **Genesis 4.11:** Now you are cursed from the ground, which has opened its mouth to receive your brother's blood from your hand.
[8] **Genesis 9.6:** Whoever sheds human blood, By man his blood shall be shed, For in the image of God He made mankind.

Conclusion

Here we have two radically different starting points for defining humanity. On one hand, we have the flexible, humanist, individual-centred reasoning of modern mainstream western society, and on the other we have reasoning based on fixed Judeo-Christian principles which leads to completely opposite conclusions.

Worldview changes everything.

According to which definition will we base our lives, our actions and our sense of right and wrong? Who is it who decides our identity? If we follow current western mainstream thinking, abortion up to birth on any grounds becomes the right of every able-bodied adult woman. Added to this must be the normalisation of assisted suicide and the imposition of the will of the stronger over the weaker in every sphere of life. This is nothing more than the logical outworking of this philosophy of what it means to be human.

But if we agree with God's definition of humanity as expressed in the Bible, we must know that we each have intrinsic worth regardless of outward appearances. This means that our children are not our property, but have been put under our authority and in our care on His behalf, and for a limited time only. This is a solemn responsibility which He gives us. So we know that to decide if our child should be allowed to live or die is not a decision which human beings have a moral right to make.

Chapter 3: What We Do: the Facts

3a: Life Before Birth: "... for the Bible Tells me so."

At what point does a person become human? Does this happen after the point of birth or at some point during pregnancy? If so, at which point in pregnancy does this transformation occur? Is there in fact no transformational moment, but rather a process or evolution towards humanity?

The Bible has much to tell us on this point. **Psalm 139** is the classic Bible text regarding the nature of the unborn.[9] According to this psalm, God was with each one of us from the time that we were in the womb, He created us there, knows us intimately from that time on, and had our whole lives planned even from that time and even though we were unseen and unknown by man at that point.

Scripture tells us that we are each unique, are known by name and have a unique calling and purpose from before birth.[10]

---

[9] **Psalm 139.11-16:** If I say, "Surely the darkness will overwhelm me... Darkness and light are alike to You. For You created my innermost parts; You wove me in my mother's womb... Because I am awesomely and wonderfully made; Wonderful are Your works... My frame was not hidden from You When I was made in secret... Your eyes have seen my formless substance; and in Your book were written All the days that were ordained for me, when as yet there was not one of them.

[10] **Isaiah 49.1:** ... The LORD called me from the womb; from the body of my mother He named me. **Isaiah 49.5:** And now says the LORD, who formed me from the womb to be His Servant, to bring Jacob back to Him,... **Jeremiah 1.5:** "Before I formed you in the womb I knew you, and before you were born I consecrated you; I have appointed you a prophet to the nations."

The Apostle Paul considered that God had "set me apart even from my mother's womb ..."[11]

The Bible tells us that from the time of being in the womb, we are capable of feeling emotion, responding to stimuli from the outside world.[12] We are even capable of being filled with the Holy Spirit during this period.[13] So from the time of being in the womb we are both physically and spiritually alive. Nowhere are we told in the Bible that this calling and identity pre-birth is only for a select few, or that it is dependent on whether we are wanted by our parents.

Various words are used for the unborn in the Bible. In **Genesis 25**, Rebekah conceives and has twins. These twins are called "children" as they struggle together in the womb.[14] The Hebrew word used here for children is "banim", the plural of "ben", which is more commonly used for children after birth, usually just meaning "sons".

In **Job 3.16**, he is suffering so much that he wishes he had never been born, saying, "Like a miscarriage which is discarded, I would not be, as infants that never saw the light." The word for "infant" here is "Olal", meaning a suckling baby or young child. This is the same word used later in **Hosea 13.16**, referring to newborn and small children.

The New Testament Greek word commonly used for the unborn is "brephos", which is used in **Luke 1.41** and then **verse 44** to refer to the unborn John the Baptist. But this word is also used in **Luke 2.12**

---

[11] **Gal 1.15**
[12] **Luke 1.44**
[13] **Luke 1.15**
[14] **Genesis 25.22**

when referring to Jesus as a born baby, **18.15** to describe how people brought their babies to Jesus to bless**,** and **Acts 7.19** to denote the babies killed by Pharaoh in Egypt.

We must conclude from this that, quite simply, the Bible makes no difference in definition between newborn babies, infants, and the unborn.

3b: "...for the Embryology Text Book tells me so."

Christian believers should look to the Bible as our source for authority and ultimate truth. But if the Bible is true, we can expect it to be confirmed by modern biology. Those who are not Christian should also be able to see that science points us back to God, and confirms the truth of Bible teaching.

So what have scientists discovered about the nature and humanity of the unborn? Let's look at the various stages of pre-born development.

Before conception: Each unfertilised egg and each male sperm contains 23 chromosomes, half of those required to make a human being.

Day 1 after conception: At the moment of egg fertilisation, or conception, the embryo contains 46 chromosomes, in other words: the complete human genome. At this moment all the future adult's inherited features, including eye and hair colour, as well as sex, have been determined.

Day 5-9: This is when implantation occurs. It is a necessary and normal change in location when the week-old embryo implants in the uterus so that it can continue to develop normally.

Day 18-20: This is when the brain begins to develop in earnest, along with the spinal cord and nervous system. This means that the building blocks for development of capacity to feel pain are being laid.

At 3 weeks: The heart beat begins to be detectable. The ears are present and the eyes begin to develop.

At 4 weeks: The arms, legs, mouth and nose begin to develop. Blood starts to flow in the veins, which is separate from the mother's blood. It can be a different blood type from the mother's. The tongue and face are present.

At 6 weeks: The brain is divided into 3 parts (again reflecting the triune nature of God in the very construction of human beings). This means that there is a capacity to experience emotion, and to process what will be seen and heard, as well as processing pain. This can be understood to be the beginning of some mental activity. Internal organs are present although immature and 99% of muscle is present with accompanying nerve supply.

At 7 weeks: We start to "breathe" oxygenated blood through the umbilical cord. In females, the ovaries are identifiable.

At 8 weeks: The liver makes blood and the kidneys start to function. Three quarters of embryos begin to exhibit right hand dominance by this time, (the rest exhibiting left-hand dominance or no preference).

This is the earliest evidence of right or left-handed behaviour. Additionally, these are the same proportions of left and right hand dominance as in the born population.

At 12 weeks: We swallow and respond to skin stimulation. Unique fingerprints are beginning to form. The latest evidence is that we are able to experience pain from at least this gestation onwards.[15]

The embryo is now called a fetus. The embryonic period is the first 12 weeks, when the basic framework of the human being is in formation, in a rudimentary stage of development. What we call the fetal period is the second 12 weeks of gestation, where the basic framework has completed formation and is now growing and developing. "Fetus" means literally "little one." These are terms which are simply a method which embryologists use for classification, but they do not signify a moment of actual transformation.

At 20 weeks: In utero surgeries for conditions such as spina bifida can be carried out at this point. Since it is recognised that the unborn experience pain by this stage in gestation, surgery involves anaesthesia.

At 24 weeks: We begin to fill the space in the womb. We are now considered "viable", meaning that the lungs and other organs are sufficiently developed for us to survive if we are born at this point,

---

[15] https://jme.bmj.com/content/46/1/3

(given adequate neonatal care).[16] Viability means that the "fetus" is now called a "baby", but again, no special transformation has occurred at this point.

At Birth: The only appreciable difference between the unborn a moment before birth, and the baby at birth, is the fact that the change in location has stimulated use of the lungs.

So, just as Scripture tells us that human life begins at conception, so biology tells us that human life begins on day one of gestation. Far from being a "blob of cells" or "tissue" as the young embryo is still frequently and incorrectly called, all the genetic information required for the future adult is present at this point in his or her development. Later development is simply confirmation of this pre-existing fact. The organs, blood supply, nervous system, facial features etc develop gradually. Although we attempt to categorise development by defining trimestral stages as "embryonic" and "fetal," it is impossible to define a transformational moment. The moment of birth is only one among many stages in development, but it is not biologically transformational. Rather, it is socially transformational, the moment when adults celebrate the arrival into the public arena of the new person who has in fact already existed for 9 months. The only time when there is a definable and radical biological change from one moment to the next, is upon conception.

---

[16] https://www.babycentre.co.uk/pregnancy-week-by-week

3c: ...Compared to Gestational Stage of Abortions

In 2019, the vast majority (82%) of abortions occurred before 10 weeks gestation in England and Wales.[17] If we refer back to the development of the unborn described in chapter 3b, we can see that this means that the vast majority of abortions, although taking place early in gestation, nevertheless occur after the unborn has developed some rudimentary capacity to feel pain, after the individual heart beat has begun to be discernable, after a separate blood flow has begun, (including separate blood type), and after a distinct and unique genetic male or female human being has begun to establish his or herself in the uterus.

Nearly 1 in 5 abortions are carried out at 7 weeks[18] at a time when the unborn also has the brain capacity to process what will be seen and heard, has internal organs (including ovaries in females), has muscles and nerve supply, and is breathing through the umbilical cord.

Nearly 1 in 5 abortions are carried out at 8 weeks' gestation. At this point an abortion is being carried out on a being who has already demonstrated enough uniqueness and personality to show a preference for the right or left hand. Nearly 1 in 10 abortions occur at

---

[17]
https://assets.publishing.service.gov.uk/government/uploads/system/uploads/attachment_data/file/891405/abortion-statistics-commentary-2019.pdf
[18]
https://assets.publishing.service.gov.uk/government/uploads/system/uploads/attachment_data/file/763174/2017-abortion-statistics-for-england-and-wales-revised.pdf

9 weeks, and roughly the same percentage occurs between 10 and 12 weeks, when the unborn is capable of responding to skin stimuli and of experience pain on some level. This is also a period when he or she has developing unique fingerprints.[19]

When a woman loses a pregnancy unintentionally during the second 12 weeks of gestation, this is called a miscarriage (meaning the loss of a fetus), but if the pregnancy is lost during the first 12 weeks, the loss of the embryo is unfortunately called a "spontaneous abortion". Although the word "abortion" is used, a spontaneous abortion is the unintentional loss of a pregnancy and is entirely different from the choice and action to end that life in an elective abortion.

According to the latest research available at the time of writing, the unborn experience pain in a way comparable to the experience of born babies from at least 12 weeks' gestation.[20] But close to 20,000 women underwent an abortion at 13 weeks or later in 2019 in England and Wales. There is no use of pain relief for the unborn during abortion at *any* gestation.

A total of 209 abortions were carried out at 24 weeks or over in 2019.[21] The legal reason given for this was "fetal abnormality" or serious threat to the woman's health. The presence of a disability or

---

19
https://assets.publishing.service.gov.uk/government/uploads/system/uploads/attachment_data/file/763174/2017-abortion-statistics-for-england-and-wales-revised.pdf
[20] https://jme.bmj.com/content/46/1/3
21
https://assets.publishing.service.gov.uk/government/uploads/system/uploads/attachment_data/file/891405/abortion-statistics-commentary-2019.pdf

abnormality does not alter the humanity of the unborn, only perhaps their likelihood of survival, possible level of suffering, along with the financial cost to the state, and heartbreak to the parents of looking after a disabled child. Threats to the woman's health are dealt with later in this book.

Conclusion

Modern science confirms what the Bible affirmed thousands of years ago: that human life begins at day one of gestation. Yet the modern practice of abortion ignores this. Therefore acceptance of abortion is based on something other than whether the unborn is a human being or not.

Chapter 4: Why We Do It: the Arguments

4a: Life Starts after Conception. Or Does it?

Many who argue the legitimacy of abortion say that human life begins at a specific point during the 9 months' gestation. Before accepting any of these definitions, we need to hold them up to scrutiny and decide if they are biologically correct, if they are logical and if so, what this says about if, or up until when abortion should be permitted.

Life starts at implantation

Increasingly in the last few decades, "conception" has been used as the term for the point 5-9 days after fertilisation, when implantation occurs. This has been used as a justification for "emergency contraception," the idea being that before this point, pregnancy has not begun. Justification for this way of defining conception is that many miscarriages (or "spontaneous abortions") occur when the unborn fails to implant. However, no special change has occurred in the embryo at this point, it is simply a change in location, another necessary stage in pregnancy. (This is discussed further in **chapter 7b**).

... when there is a heartbeat

In **chapter 3b** we saw how modern science has demonstrated that the unborn have a measurable heart beat almost before the mother knows she is pregnant (day 21), and it may be that in the future, scientists will be able to detect the fetal heart beat at an even earlier stage.

Adults who have had a heart attack etc can be kept alive using machines, but they are still considered to be alive even though they do not have an independent heart beat. So if we consider terminating the life of an adult on life support to be murder, the absence of perceivable heartbeat on the part of the unborn cannot be legitimate justification for termination of that life.

... when the person is breathing

Even some Christians say that since God breathed His life into Adam, and only then was he alive, all life begins with the first breath of oxygen.

The unborn begins to breathe (through the umbilical cord) at 7 weeks' gestation. If we follow the logic that life begins when we start to breathe, abortion must not be permitted beyond 7 weeks.

Adults who cannot breathe on their own can be kept alive using a ventilator, but they are still considered to be alive. The Biblical Adam was a special case since he neither had a mother nor was ever an embryo, so he cannot be used as a model for the rest of mankind. If we were to accept the argument that Adam is our model in this sense, then all human life must only start when we become adult. So this is clearly not a logical argument.

… when there is mental activity[22]

There is some discussion over when mental activity begins. Referring back to our timetable of development, mental activity can be said to begin development at around 2 and a half weeks when the brain, spinal cord and nerves begin development, or it could be contended that it starts at around 6 weeks when we know that the brain is divided into its three parts. Embryologists are coming more and more to the point of considering that mental activity begins at around 12 weeks when it is assessed that the unborn is capable of experiencing pain in the same way as born infants. Either way, this definition would mean that beyond 3 months of gestation, abortion should not be permissible. It would also mean that the life of an adult in a persistent vegetative state, who does not have mental activity, has no intrinsic value either.

"*Sentience*" (which is linked to mental activity) is a term used to describe the moment a person begins to feel, think and experience subjectively, to know he or she is a "person". This is not a scientific concept but rather a philosophical one which rests on the science of fetal mental activity. There is no consensus in this area of research.

Psychologists assert that a baby of between 6 and 9 months of age (after birth) begins to realise that he or she is a separate person from their mother.[23] The baby may begin to have attachment issues with his or her mother at this point. It could be argued, according to this logic, that sentience begins 6-9 months *after* birth, so logically, a

---

[22] https://www.princeton.edu/~prolife/articles/wdhbb.html
[23] https://healthywa.wa.gov.au/Articles/A_E/Child-development-6-9-months

baby might not be considered human until after this point. Further, as the philosopher and research biochemist Dianne N Irving states: "The scientific fact is that the brain, which is supposed to be the physiological support for *both* "rational attributes" *and* "sentience," is not actually completely developed until young adulthood".[24] Thus to carry this to its logical conclusion, to the normalisation of abortion should be added the legalisation of infanticide and justification of murder of people up until young adulthood. If we doubt that this is a reasonable attitude to have towards babies, children and young adults, then perhaps we should question the rationality of having this attitude towards the unborn.

If we decide that being a "person" depends on one's rational attributes and "sentience," other groups with diminished rational attributes should not be considered human or worthy of protection either. This list would include the mentally ill, the mentally disabled, the depressed elderly, Alzheimer's and Parkinson's patients, drug addicts and alcoholics, comatose patients, people in a persistent vegetative state, paraplegics, and other paralysed and disabled patients or other patients with nerve or brain damage.[25]

It is argued that sentience, in turn, leads to the development of the ability to *suffer and feel pain*. The argument is that under a certain gestation, the unborn cannot feel pain because of a lack of brain development. The logic of defining humanity by ability to experience pain is questionable since we know that someone who is in chronic

---

[24] https://www.princeton.edu/~prolife/articles/wdhbb.html
[25] ibid

pain is not more human or more alive than someone who is incapable of feeling pain. In any case, pain is a notoriously difficult phenomenon to quantify, even for the adult human. Because we are unable to communicate with the very young, we have traditionally supposed that newborns and young infants do not experience pain as much as adults. This assumption been has proved to be wrong.[26] Similarly with the unborn, we have seen that the latest research indicates that response to pain can be detected from at least the 12th week of gestation.[27] There is also a lack of pain inhibition mechanisms which means that the perception of pain may in fact be greater in the human before birth than in an adult. There is evidence that from the 15th week of gestation the unborn are extremely sensitive to painful stimuli.[28] It has also been discovered that at the moment the unborn of 28-34 weeks' gestation receive the anaesthetic injection before intrauterine surgery, they exhibit changes in facial expression similar to newborn babies experiencing pain.[29] We must conclude that there is ample evidence that the unborn experience pain.

If sentience leads to personhood and the ability to experience pain, this would imply that adult groups of people with impaired mental capacity are not capable of feeling pain either, and are not in fact "people". According to this rationale, the unborn are at least as human and can feel at least as much pain as people who have diminished rational attributes.

---

[26] https://pmj.bmj.com/content/79/934/438
[27] https://jme.bmj.com/content/46/1/3
[28] https://www.pubmed.ncbi.nlm.nih.gov/27881927
[29] Sorting pain out of salience: assessment of pain facial expressions in the human fetus (nih.gov)

We are unlikely ever to know what the unborn think about themselves. We also have to ask what pain has to do with humanity. Animals feel pain yet are not human. In 1997 the concept of animal sentience was written into the basic law of the EU. Member states must therefore "pay regard to the welfare requirements of animals"[30]. It appears that sentience is brought into the abortion debate because the welfare of animals is now considered to be at least on the same level as the welfare of unborn humans. Added to this, if animals are protected, no matter their age due to their sentience yet the unborn are not protected because they are said to lack sentience, we must accept the undeniable fact that modern society values and protects animals more than it protects unborn human beings. Is this acceptable to us and something which we are content to leave unchallenged?

So taking all these things into account, we must conclude that whether the unborn feel pain or not is as irrelevant to their humanity as it is to the humanity of any adult.

Abortion providers are reluctant to acknowledge that the unborn feel pain even though the evidence for it is accepted by those who perform in utero surgery. The reluctance is not because of any medical reason, but because this would mean an acknowledgement that the unborn are vulnerable human beings who require protection. Biology therefore tells us that abortion involves another human being who is being denied their right to life and is in pain (from at least the 12th week of gestation) whilst their life is being ended.

---

[30] https://www.ciwf.org.uk/media/3818623/eu-law-on-the-welfare-of-farm-animals.pdf

... when the unborn can live independently

The age at which the unborn are capable of living independently of the mother is generally taken to be around 24 weeks' gestation. The legal limit for abortion in the UK is 24 weeks precisely because of this idea. But in practice the gestation at which the unborn can survive outside the womb depends heavily on where the mother lives. In the developed world, a baby can survive outside the womb in some cases from about 20 or 21 weeks' gestation. In the developing world, however, and where health care is less advanced, the unborn needs to be much more developed to survive independently. So if we look at the logic of considering the beginning of human life to be when the unborn are able to survive independently of the mother, this would mean the humanity of the unborn depends on where their mother lives. It would mean that premature babies born in the wealthy West are more human than those born in the developing world.

Where do we draw the line of what constitutes dependence? A child is not fully independent until adulthood, so if we are to conclude this logic, infanticide must be permissible up until adulthood. This means that we are a society which discriminates against people on the grounds of age, which only values the right of the stronger over the weaker. This is far from being a modern and advanced framework of thinking. Humanity is not defined by independence.

4b: Personhood

We have seen that from the point of conception, the unborn is both human and alive. We could say that this means that those human beings should be protected, just as children are protected from abusive parents, and the marginalised protected from discrimination and bullying.

Yet it is commonly argued that even so, abortion is morally allowable. This is because "the fetus is not a person". This is a philosophical concept, not a scientific one, asserting that to be a "person" is much more than mere DNA and potential for future life outside the womb. It has to do with self-awareness, self-determination and the person's awareness of having a future and a past. Many accept that the unborn are human life but simply deny that they have any rights when compared to that of the grown woman to decide whether she wants the child or not.

Since this is not a scientific argument, what is it based on? The unborn are hidden from our view for 9 months. Only in the last few decades have we been able to have the occasional glimpse of them through ultrasound. It is still mainly the case that we do not see the unborn themselves, only the signs of their presence. The very young unborn do not appear human at all, and even once quite developed, lack many of the qualities which we think of as attractive (having elongated head and hands, gelatinous skin etc). The unborn are also unable to communicate with us. So this argument of "personhood" is based on our perception, what we see and hear and how we respond emotionally to the unborn. According to this argument, the unborn, up until the point we consider them to be a "person" are human life, but of a lesser value.

Of course, this argument appeals to changeable emotions and opinions rather than any fixed fact. We will ascribe value to the unborn according to our own emotions around the pregnancy, and this will depend if the child is wanted or not. And this view rests neatly on the evolutionary world view, there being no moment of transformation from nothing to full humanity. Rather, from the point of conception, there is a sliding scale of value up until birth. Ernst Haeckel's theory of recapitulation in the womb lends itself to this idea.[31] This theory states that the development of the individual embryo repeats its alleged evolutionary history, going through stages where it has gills like a fish, a tail like a monkey etc, until the time when it is fully human and ready for birth. So, just as man is on a sliding scale of value from his ancient ancestors to the present day, the unborn are to be valued in the same way. (The infamous theory of embryonic recapitulation has been known for many years to be completely erroneous).

The idea that the unborn are human but "less human" than the born, therefore having lesser human rights, is in effect, to view them as subhuman. This principle is similar to the racist views which underpinned acceptance of African slavery, apartheid and the Holocaust. The only difference is that discrimination is here not based on race but on age.

---

[31] https://embryo.asu.edu/pages/ernst-haeckels-biogenetic-law-1866

Although the young embryo does not look human, he or she (the sex has already by this time been determined) looks how he or she is meant to look, and how we all looked at that age. Abnormal humans like Joseph Merrick (the Elephant Man), are nevertheless human, regardless of how they look. African slavery was accepted in centuries past, partly because we were unfamiliar with the appearance of black human beings, so we simply looked at the outward appearance and made moral judgments on them based on this superficial and ignorant understanding of what it means to be human.

We are commonly told that science and logic prove that abortion is an ethical option. It is also commonly asserted that arguments in defence of the unborn are based on emotion. But when we consider all these justifications for abortion in the light of human biology and basic logic, they are revealed to be erroneous, unscientific and emotionally-based.

Conclusion

It is common to hear that the unborn are not human, but this assertion requires evidence. To separate the essence of humanity from his or her ability is to improperly define humanity. A person is still a person if he cannot think, walk or be self-aware.

To state that a life is not a human life at a certain stage in gestation, and then is a human life at a later stage, requires evidence of radical transformation. The only point at which this radical change happens is at conception, before which the genetic information required to make a unique individual was *not* there, and after which *everything* about our genetic makeup was there.

In order to accept the pro-abortion argument, we have to ignore the evidence of ultrasound and neo-natal survival of babies born at an earlier and earlier gestation. We must ignore numerous great advances in antenatal obstetric surgery, genetic medicine and numerous other advances, all of which provide less and less clinical grounds for non-therapeutic abortion.

We can see from this that far from the pro-life argument drawing on the emotional, it is based on solid scientific fact, and it is in fact the "Pro-choice" argument which is both unscientific and illogical, drawing on nebulous philosophical and emotional arguments which can be demonstrated to hold no water.

The logical consequence of defining when life begins at a certain point during gestation is to push the boundaries of what constitutes humanity. Since there is no special distinction between the unborn and the newborn, and since we question the humanity of the unborn, we must begin to question the humanity of the newborn. And if the unborn human simply has the "potential" to become a valuable human being, then we should by the same logic say that a small child should only be valued according to the "potential" he or she has of becoming an adult. The bio-ethicist and philosopher, Peter Singer takes the logical next step of supporting infanticide, saying that "Newborn infants, especially if not wanted, are not yet fully-blown members of the moral community".[32] He is not alone in this

---

[32] Singer, P., *Rethinking Life and Death: The Collapse of Our Traditional*

assessment. The "ethics experts" Giubilini and Minerva make a similar argument in their 2012 medical article: "After-birth abortion: why should the baby live?"[33] This justification for infanticide is simply the logical outcome of arbitrarily deciding when a "fetus" becomes a "baby" whose life is worthy of protection. The logical outcome of questioning the humanity of the unborn will also be a questioning of the humanity of other unfavoured groups like the elderly, disabled and eventually the unintelligent and whoever else we decide is of lesser value than others. We must have the courage to face the final outcome of the logic of our thinking, and then decide if perhaps the conclusion indicates that our starting point was wrong.

Finally, if life in the womb is of lesser value then there can be no guilt in terminating that life, just as there is no guilt involved in any other surgery. So the fact that guilt is such a fundamental problem for so many women who go through an abortion indicates that we already know at what point humanity begins.

Ethics, pp. 130, 217. New York: Prometheus Booklets, 1995; quoted in: Flynn, D. *Intellectual Morons: How Ideology Makes Smart People Fall for Stupid Ideas,* p. 74. New York: Crown Forum, 2004.
[33] https://jme.bmj.com/content/39/5/261

4c: Adult-Centred Reasons

Once we decide that the unborn are entirely human and alive, there can be no justification for abortion. So the onus is on those who justify abortion to demonstrate that the unborn are not human or alive. Otherwise abortion must be seen as reckless, like a hunter shooting in the bushes not knowing if there is a living human being there or not.

Modern discourse tends to focus the debate on a woman's right to choose because it is impossible to refute the humanity of the unborn, either scientifically or philosophically.

Here are some common adult-centred justifications for abortion along with analysis of the validity of these arguments:

Abortion is legal

Legality is not a moral or ethical justification for anything. Governments have a moral responsibility towards their citizens, but what a particular government allows us to do is not necessarily moral. At times in the world's history, slavery has been legal, as well as racial segregation (apartheid) and mass killing of Jews. Infanticide has been the norm and at least tolerated by many cultures throughout history. Yet this does not make infanticide morally justifiable. However, since abortion is legal on request in most of the northern hemisphere, it is considered by many to be morally justifiable. If we are against slavery, racism, infanticide and the holocaust, then this is not a coherent point of view.

Life in the womb is part of the woman

We have seen that at the very point of conception, there exists inside the woman's body, a separate and distinct body, with separate DNA, then possibly a separate blood type, separate arms and legs. So the unborn is patently and obviously not part of the woman's body but is only *located* there, and reliant on her body for survival. Since the unborn is a biologically separate human being from the moment of conception, we cannot reasonably describe abortion as being simply the "the removal of a pregnancy," as it is euphemistically described on the websites of our major abortion providers. To describe it in this way is like describing the actions of the 9/11 hijackers as "deciding to terminate their flight." This would only be true if they were the only ones affected, and if the termination did not involve death.

The idea that the unborn are only a part of the woman, and consequently that the adult woman alone accords the unborn with value, is comparable to ideas faced historically by slaves in the USA. The argument of the slave-owner was that if his slave was *on his own property*, then this meant that the owner had the right to decide the slave's value, whether he was human or not and even whether he should live or die. The rights of the slave belonged not to the slave but to the slave's owner.

Those who decide that the value of human life is not intrinsic must come to the same conclusion regarding the unborn: If human rights are based on location and whether the person is currently reliant on another for survival, then we should support slavery as being part of the human rights of the slave owner. But those who disagree with inhumane treatment of human beings once we *call* them slaves, should conclude that having this attitude towards the unborn once we *call* them "fetus" or "embryo" is equally immoral.

The woman's right to choose

This is one of the most common arguments to justify abortion. More specifically, words to the effect that: "If you disagree with abortion, don't have one. But don't tell other women what to do with their body."

We must remember that it is not the adult woman's body which is aborted. Your freedom and my freedom to do what we wish with our own body stops where someone else's body begins, and certainly does not include the right to terminate that other person's body.

According to the freedom of choice argument, adult happiness and comfort are weighed against, and placed above the fundamental right to life of the unborn. We deny a woman the right to steal for her own benefit, and even for the benefit of her remaining family, since to steal is an infringement of the rights of another person, regardless of our reasons. To say that an adult has the moral right to end the life of an unborn human being is to say that might is right: this is again the law of the jungle.

So abortion has never been about "choice". In great part, it is about escaping the consequences of choices made by adults by taking away the "choices" of the most innocent among us.

Logically, we must conclude that justifying abortion on the grounds of free choice for women is the result of a process of dehumanization of the unborn, because factually, we are dealing with a young human being rather than a choice.

Since the humanity of the unborn has been demonstrated, let's take a look at the logical culmination of focussing on the woman's right to choose. By substituting a 2-year-old living human being for the unborn living human being, we can assess how some of the common justifications for abortion sound:

1) I have a right to choose to kill a disruptive 2-year-old.
2) It is the right of every 2-year-old to be wanted.
3) No one forces you to kill your 2-year-old.
4) I am not pro-killing 2-year-olds, I am pro-choice.
5) We want killing 2-year-olds to be safe, legal and rare.
6) If we make a law against this, those who are rich enough will just hire a hit-man to kill the 2-year-old , while the poor can't do this so such laws are discriminatory against the poor.
7) Unless you're prepared to adopt this child you have no right to tell the mother that she shouldn't kill her 2-year-old.
8) If we don't make it possible for a mother to kill her 2-year-old safely, she will do it in ways that aren't safe and may put her own health in danger.
9) It is "speciesist" to give human 2-year-olds more protection than a 2-year-old chimpanzee.

10) Those who are opposed to killing 2-year-olds are religious fanatics.

11) If the 2-year-old is the product of incestuous rape then its existence is a constant reminder to the mother of what happened to her so she should be allowed to kill it.

12) Stem cells could be harvested from the 2-year-old to help cure many horrible diseases. Religious fanatics want to stop this valuable scientific research.[34]

Philosophers and ethicists such as Peter Singer underpin common arguments in favour of abortion. They are society's opinion-leaders, and for this reason, if unchallenged, eventually influence government policy. The person who justifies abortion may not be willing to go as far as Singer in advocating infanticide, yet we must be willing to accept the logical outcome of our arguments, then decide for ourselves if abortion along with infanticide should therefore be acceptable to society or not. If humanity begins at conception, however, these adult-centred arguments are revealed to be irrelevant and incorrect as well as shockingly contemptuous of the intrinsic value of human life.

**"I notice that everyone who is for abortion
Has already been born." Ronald Reagan**

---

[34] Politically Correct Death by Dr Francis Beckwith Baker Booklets, Grand Rapids, MI, 1993, quoted in the booklet review:
https://creation.com/antidote-to-abortion-arguments

Chapter 5: Contrasting Attitudes

We have discovered up to this point, that whether we consider abortion to be acceptable depends on whether we consider humanity to be special, and if so at what point in gestation that specialness starts. We have also seen some of the logical consequences of that reasoning. Let's return to the Biblical source of Christian thinking and see how this compares to modern popular thinking on abortion. In **Ecclesiastes 11.5** we see that the God who made the unimaginably enormous majesty of the universe, also made the darkened privacy of the womb.[35] Although man may understand some things about both, and we often behave as if we knew everything, in fact both the universe and the womb are ultimately a mystery to us. The most knowledgeable and skilled surgeons, as well as the most knowledgeable astronomers, recognise this as obvious fact. This gives some indication of the distance between the level of understanding of human beings, and that of God. It also gives some indication of the arrogance of human beings when we destroy that work.

How do the actions of God compare to those of human beings? God humbled Himself to the point of becoming a man. Not just a man, but a baby, and not just a baby but an embryo, meaning a single dividing cell.[36] He inhabited our fundamental identity, reflecting back

---

[35] Just as you do not know the path of the wind and how bones are formed in the womb of the pregnant woman, so you do not know the activity of God who makes all things.

[36] **Philippians 2.6-8:** ... He already existed in the form of God, did not consider equality with God something to be grasped, but emptied Himself by taking the form of a bond-servant and being born in the likeness

to us the fact that we are made in His image. He comes down to our human level to raise us up to His.

If we consider for a moment the Fall of mankind in **Genesis 3,** we find that the serpent's temptation of Eve involved the idea of obtaining wisdom to become like God. But what the serpent did not explain is that this wisdom, attained through disobedience to God, would necessarily be "worldly wisdom" which would, (perhaps imperceptibly but inevitably) lead away from God and therefore away from life.

The purpose of Satan is the same today as it was in the Garden of Eden and throughout Scripture: to steal, kill and destroy.[37] So wisdom obtained by following his plan, even if it appears benign and perhaps beneficial to us, since it ultimately comes from a satanic source is totally contrary to the wisdom of God. Wisdom which is independent of God, may lead us to obtain many good things, so we assume that it must be good. But the serpent remains cunning and deceptive today. Once the wisdom of this world has achieved great things according to our understanding, it eventually leads down a dark path. This satanic deception eventually causes us to rationalise and justify the idea that we are "like God" in the sense that we are capable of choosing if another person's life is valid. We end up thinking that it is our place to decide if that other person should live or die. The final destination and ultimate goal of this wisdom obtained through disobedience to God, is that we think it our place to decide the value of another

---

of men. And being found in appearance as a man, He humbled Himself by becoming obedient to the point of death: death on a cross. [ESV]
[37] **John 10.10**

person. A key example of this is found in the abortion industry which tells us that it is a woman's role to ascribe value to her unborn child. This is totally contrary to the wisdom of God.

In the parable of the sheep and the goats (**Matthew 25.31-46)** we read how on the day of judgement, we will be separated into two groups: those who have demonstrated their love for God by helping others who were in difficulty, and those who have demonstrated their rejection of Him by not helping others who were in difficulty, such as the poor, the sick and people in prison. Both those who are accepted and those who are rejected by God in this parable express surprise that they have been judged according to how they treated these despised members of society. Jesus answers, "Truly I say to you, to the extent that you did it to one of these brothers of mine, even the least of them, you did it to Me".[38] Jesus actually identifies Himself with this group of outcasts, considering that what is done to them is in fact done to Him. Surely, the "very least of these brothers" would include those whose very existence is denied, those who are discarded by our society and whose humanity is routinely dismissed: the unborn.

Human beings naturally judge each other according to how we treat the most powerful and respected in society. This is something that can be seen and approved by others and we expect to be respected in return. But in God's eyes, the genuineness of our faith is assessed according to how we treat those who are despised and dismissed by arrogant man, but those who are nevertheless valued by

---

[38] **Matt. 25.40**

God because they too are made in His image. In fact, it could be argued that the unborn are more in the image of God than adult human beings, since they are innocent of sin. Jesus identified Himself with these human beings as much as with the rest of us when He took our place on the cross. He took their place too.

In the light of this, should we ever consider it a woman's right to choose abortion even if the circumstances are challenging or heart-breaking? The capacity to have a baby should not be taken for granted, as anyone who is unable to have children will tell us. When the Angel Gabriel told Mary that she would become pregnant with Jesus, the stigma and even the risk of being stoned to death that went with pregnancy outside marriage, did not deter her from responding to this by humbly submitting to the will of God.[39] The ramifications of this are enormous. Our Salvation began because of this willingness to face an uncertain and stigmatised future, perhaps death, simply because God asked.

Thus we see that the protection of the unborn, far from being a side issue to the Gospel message, is fundamental to how God treats us. And just as our spiritual and emotional life belong to God, so does our physical body.[40]

---

[39] **Luke 1.38:** …. "Behold, the Lord's bond-servant; may it be done to me according to your word."

[40] **Galatians 2.20:** "I have been crucified with Christ; and it is no longer I who live, but Christ lives in me…"

Just as our children do not belong to us, so our own body is not ours to do with as we please, since it has been bought at a price (See **chapter 1B, "Restoration"** p.113).

Chapter 6: Murder of Innocents

The Bible tells us that murder is wrong. It specifically condemns the murder of innocents.[41] In order to receive the Good News that there is forgiveness for *all* people and for *every* sin when we repent before Christ, we have to recognise what sin *is*. Then we have to recognise the extent of the bad news, which is the consequence of that sin, and what is its just punishment.

Scripture tells us that God judges without exception *all* those who are guilty of shedding innocent blood.[42] When an innocent person is killed, even if no one knows about it, their blood has a voice before God, crying out for justice. God knows when an injustice has been perpetrated and He requires justice.[43] He calls the shedding of innocent blood an abomination.[44] The righteous penalty for this sin is death and separation from God.[45] This is the basic law of God's justice, which may seem harsh, but it is there to protect the innocent and the weak. His righteousness is *part of* His love.

During the slavery of the Israelites in Egypt, the Jewish midwives were told to put to death any newborn boys.[46] But the Bible carefully

---

[41] **Exodus 23.7a:** Keep far from a false charge, and do not kill the innocent or the righteous…

[42] **Exodus 23.7b**

[43] **Genesis 4.10:** [God] said, "What have you done? The voice of your brother's blood is crying to Me from the ground.

[44] **Proverbs 6.16-18:** There are six things that the LORD hates, Seven that are an abomination to Him: Haughty eyes, a lying tongue, And hands that shed innocent blood, A heart that devises wicked plans, Feet that run rapidly to evil.

[45] **Deuteronomy 19.11-13**

[46] **Exodus 1:15-16**

records that the midwives "feared God" and would not do it.[47] We are told that we must fear God more than we fear the consequences of going against human laws which breach the law of God.

Possibly the most infamous murder of innocents in the Bible was that of Herod, King of Judea at around the time of Jesus' birth. When he heard of the birth of someone he supposed to be a rival for his position as King of the Jews, Herod, unable to find his real target, ordered the slaughter of all the young children in the region of Bethlehem.[48] We can clearly see from this that the inevitable response of evil when confronted by holiness is the urge to extinguish, blot out and destroy it. Concerned only with his status, power base and political position, Herod targeted defenceless children who happened to be in the wrong place at the wrong time. This was the case regarding political leaders in biblical times, and the principle remains true today where there is fear of man but no fear of God.

The God of the Bible is perfect in righteousness and requires justice. He is particularly concerned with protection of the most vulnerable and most innocent. But without compromising that requirement, He is also merciful to us, (see **chapter 1B, "Restoration"** p.113).

---

[47] **Exodus 1:17**
[48] **Matthew 2.16-18**

Chapter 7: Ancient and Modern Practice

(Comparing Ancient Practices Recorded in
The Bible with Modern Thought on Abortion)

7a: Abortion, Sacrifice in the Bible

The Bible as well as biology make it clear that the unborn are completely human and there is no fundamental difference between them and the newly born. For this reason, the practice of abortion can be compared to the ancient practice of infanticide.

Infanticide has been seen as a kind of birth control in many parts of the world throughout history including Ancient Greece and Rome, pagan Europe, pre-Columbian North and South America, Ancient China, Japan and India. Often infanticide was to rid a group of the weak and deformed or it was due to poverty, cultural preference for boys or social stigma such as birth out of wedlock. But infanticide was also often seen as a way to ensure health, good fortune, and general fertility. It was prohibited in only a few societies, notably the Hebrew culture, then under Christianity and later under Islam. In all cases the prohibition was due to religious teaching and the practice diminished in proportion to the spread of the religion. In modern societies, frequency of infanticide has greatly reduced due to availability of effective contraception and abortion.

Infanticide was common among the nations surrounding Ancient Israel. The Old Testament refers many times to child sacrifice to the pagan god Molech, (also called Moloch, Milcom or Milcam), when a person killed their child in sacrifice, "giving" him or her to Molech by "passing him or her through the fire" in propitiation, in the hopes of appeasing this god or gaining prosperity. It was carried out in the Valley of Topheth, (also known as the Valley of Hinnom, or the Valley of Slaughter). This was one of the practices of the Canaanites which God forbade His people from participating in.[49]

Leviticus 20.2-5 gives a more detailed explanation of how God viewed child sacrifice. His condemnation of child sacrifice was because it was in marked contrast to the sanctity of life expressed throughout His Word. We know that the children of the Israelites were considered by God to be *His* children rather than being the property of their parents to do with as they wished.[50] Notice that the prohibition of the sacrifice of children to Molech found in Leviticus 18 is part of a detailed list of prohibited sexual practices. There was a spiritual connection between sexual sin and child sacrifice.

The sacrifice of infants to Molech was seen as the culmination of the wickedness of a nation.[51] It also was associated with occult satanic practices.[52]

---

[49] **Leviticus 18.21:** You shall not give any of your offspring to offer them to Molech, Nor shall you profane the name of your God; I am the LORD.

[50] **Ezekiel 16:20-21**: "Furthermore, you took your sons and daughters whom you had borne to Me and sacrificed them to idols to be devoured. Were your obscene practices a trivial matter? You slaughtered My children and offered them to idols by making them pass through the fire.

[51] **Deuteronomy 12:31:** ...every abominable act which the LORD hates they have done for their gods; for they even burn their sons and daughters in the fire for their gods.

[52] **Deuteronomy 18:10-12:** There shall not be found among you anyone who makes his son or his daughter pass through the fire, one who uses

Punishment for sacrifice to Molech was death. Judgement was also to be against the family of the perpetrator. Later, we find that the Israelites were disobedient to this command.[53]

Child sacrifice was practiced and promoted by kings such as Ahaz and Manasseh.[54]

As a consequence, child sacrifice became a common thing, accepted by the nation as a whole. When Josiah brought Judah back to God, he destroyed the places where these sacrifices were carried out.[55]

But the practice revived and continued until the fall of Jerusalem, giving some indication of how much this practice had become such a normalised and integral part of the culture that it was apparently extremely difficult to eradicate. It was perhaps as normalised as abortion is in Britain, including within the church today.

---

divination, a soothsayer, one who interprets omens, or a sorcerer, or one who casts a spell, or a medium, or a spiritist, or one who consults the dead. For whoever does these things is detestable to the LORD....

[53] **1 Kings 11.7:** Then Solomon built a high place ... for Molech the detestable idol of the sons of Ammon.. **Jeremiah 32.35:** They built the high places of Baal that are in the Valley of Ben-hinnom to make their sons and their daughters pass through the fire to Molech, which I had not commanded them, nor had it entered My mind that they should do this abomination, to mislead Judah to sin.

[54] **2 kings 16.3. 2 kings 21.6:** And he made his son pass through the fire, interpreted signs, practiced divination, and used mediums and spiritists. He did great evil in the sight of the LORD, provoking Him to anger.

[55] **2 Kings 23.10**

7b: Modern "Altars" of Sacrifice

We may think that abortion is completely different in nature from child sacrifice in ancient times, and that our reasons for abortion are not a sacrifice to a blood-thirsty idol. This may be firstly because we consider the unborn to be different in nature to a born baby. But we have seen that this is not so, either biologically, or according to Bible teaching. Secondly, we may believe that abortion is a necessity and choice rather than a pagan sacrifice. However we will see that this is not the case either.

We live in a fallen world where families, marriages, relationships and finances are not always stable. But let's make no mistake here: this was also the case in times when abortion was illegal, stigmatised and rare. People down the ages have found themselves cornered by their own actions, the actions of others, and circumstances, into a situation where the only solution apparent is to have an abortion. So abortion is a consequence of living in a sinful world and having our understanding steeped in sin. But once we have established that the unborn are human and alive from conception, we have to conclude that abortion is child sacrifice in modern times just as it was in ancient times. The only difference is the particular reason, or the "altar" upon which the "sacrifice" occurs.

Some examples of modern-day "altars"

Fear

In 2019, 98% of abortions were carried out under statutory grounds C[56], the main reason given being that there is a risk to the health of the woman if the pregnancy were not terminated. Since most pregnancies are healthy, and are not a threat to the *physical* health of the woman, the threat must be to the *mental* health of the woman. One major reason for this would be fear: "How will I (or we) cope?" "What will people think?" etc. This has always been a reason for abortion, but in other eras the fear of the dangers involved in abortion, as well as the stigma, and also the fear of God, were often greater than the fear of having the child in adverse circumstances. There can be fear because the woman's relationship has already ended, leading to a lack of emotional and financial stability. Another cause for fear which has been underplayed by proponents of abortion is the fear caused by an abusive partner who does not want a child, or wants to hide the evidence of an abusive situation by preventing the birth of a child.

Lifestyle

This is where the arrival of a child, or the kind of child we think he or she will be, does not match the parents' aspirations. If the parent(s) want a boy but the child is a girl (or occasionally vice versa,) abortion

---

[56]

https://assets.publishing.service.gov.uk/government/uploads/system/uploads/attachment_data/file/891405/abortion-statistics-commentary-2019.pdf

might be considered. The "altar" is lifestyle choice usually based on misogyny.

Perhaps the unborn is found to have some defect which does not match the parents' dreams of family. Although sometimes the diagnosis of fetal abnormality can indicate that the unborn has very poor prospects for life, this is extremely rare. Abnormalities which are routinely quoted as legitimate reasons for abortion up to birth include Down's syndrome.

Currently in the UK, 90% of the unborn who are given a definite diagnosis of Down's syndrome are aborted.[57] Up until recently, it was not possible to know if a child had Downs until the baby was born, but it is claimed that the 'non-invasive' prenatal blood test gives parents a 99% indication of the Down's status of their unborn child. This test is being heavily promoted throughout the world, but its use is problematic since it goes against the 1968 World Health Organisation guideline criteria which state that population-wide screening is only acceptable if a "treatment for patients with the disease" is available. Since Down's syndrome is a genetic condition rather than a disease and there is no "cure" for it, the increasingly widespread practice of prenatal blood testing has been condemned as "eugenic" by human rights campaigners.[58]

This is evidence that the label of "fetal abnormality" has come to mean that perfectly survivable disabilities are now considered

---

[57] https://dontscreenusout.org/wp-content/uploads/2016/02/Abortion-and-Disability-Report-17-7-13.pdf
[58] https://adfinternational.org/news/down-syndrome-is-becoming-a-death-sentence/

reasonable justification for abortion. This creates a deeply negative impression around disability in a culture which otherwise works hard to ensure that people who are disabled are not discriminated against. We have a society which prohibits discrimination based on disability in the outside world but which allows, and even encourages it in the womb, often treating those who decide not to abort as being "irresponsible parents." The definition of fetal abnormality has been stretched so that there have been cases of late term abortions due to fetal cleft lip or club foot[59], which are both perfectly remediable fetal abnormalities. In an increasing number of instances, the label of fetal abnormality has become a pretext, feeding into the "designer-baby" culture. Additionally, this means that we cannot be taken seriously when we insist that as a society we value and care for the disabled.

---

[59] https://www.telegraph.co.uk/news/politics/10183668/MPs-Abortions-being-carried-out-for-cleft-palates.html

Finance, career or education

An abortion may be considered because pregnancy is seen to threaten a woman's current or future career prospects. Women now expect career and financial independence which they may not believe to be compatible with having a child at an unexpected time or when there is no father in the picture to share the responsibility. A woman's financial independence and career are not negative aspirations, but we must recognise the reality that sacrifices are made quite literally to achieve these things.

There can also be urgent financial necessity. Aiming to have enough to provide for our needs is a good and necessary thing, and this is not to minimise the impact of negative circumstances in which women (and men) can find themselves. The point is to recognise the reasons that decisions are made.

Throughout history, before contraception was widely available, an unplanned pregnancy was a normal and expected thing, something which had to be coped with in one way or another. Before the arrival of the Welfare State, this very often meant dire poverty for the whole family, and sometimes women had an illegal abortion. But abortion was still illegal and stigmatised because the unborn was considered to be human. (Hence the archaic term for pregnancy: being "with child").

We are a far wealthier society today than in eras when abortion was illegal, and we do not aim to return to times of widespread poverty. We consider part of the role of the state to be to provide for the needs of families during times of difficulty, and we have charities to fill the gap where government fails in this. In addition, it should be possible for widely available cheap contraception to prevent most unwanted pregnancies.

At the end of the day, money issues are an "altar" upon which the unborn are sacrificed.

Sexual sin

The following is not a condemnation of any person; rather it is an explanation of the consequences of our actions and the consequences of what have become cultural norms.

A central theme of the Bible is that God's plan was for one (biological) man and one (biological) woman to come together as one flesh in committed, lifelong marriage. The purpose of this was not for the adult individuals to find satisfaction or for the couple to find happiness and fulfilment in each other, although this would be a consequence. Marriage needn't necessarily produce children but the fundamental original and practical purpose for it was so that both man and woman together took full responsibility for any possible outcome of their physical union. The purpose was a commitment to the secure upbringing of their children. The key phrase here is "taking responsibility for the consequences of our actions."

Reasons for social change are complex and interdependent, and I do not want to over-simplify. We have nevertheless seen in the last fifty years a radical change in marriage and relationships in the West. In the UK, this metamorphosis has taken place over the same period that abortion has become more and more normalised, against a background of contraception becoming widely available and since the cultural influence on British society of Judeo-Christian values has also markedly declined. There has been a gradual long-term decline in marriage since 1972, with a corresponding rise in cohabitation.[60] During the same period in history when sex outside of marriage has become the cultural norm, the institution of marriage has weakened in our society. This has in turn compromised the protective structure of the family, as indicated by the percentage of lone parent families in the UK - nearly 15% in 2019, which equates to nearly 3 million families.[61] (This is of course not a judgement on those 3 million families, but simply a factual observation of the consequences of changes in cultural norms).

Marital life in previous generations was clearly not perfect and was open to abuse since human beings have always been flawed. But we have to be aware that factually there is widespread non-conformity to biblical laws on sex within marriage only. The inevitable consequence of this is that there has been a separation in our minds of the sexual act from the expectation of procreation. This may not be what we like to hear but basic biology tells us that women are designed to get pregnant when they have sex. This is the only biological reason that the sexual act exists. Modern society has separated the two things, however, making sex a recreational act with an option on commitment. It has become an expression of freedom to be practiced under whichever circumstances its participants deem

---

[60] Marriages in England and Wales - Office for National Statistics (ons.gov.uk)
[61] Families and households in the UK - Office for National Statistics (ons.gov.uk)

reasonable, "consent" being the only limiter. The sexual act has not only been separated from procreation, it has become separated from the notion of relationship and has become an end in itself. It is no coincidence that this change in attitudes coincides with a period in history which has seen untold proliferation of pornography and the objectification and sexualisation of women, with a consequent separation, in our thinking, of the "person" from the body. This objectification of women has led to further weakening of the institution of marriage in society so that family stability has been eroded, as indicated by the fact that 4 out of 5 abortions were carried out on unmarried women in England and Wales in 2019.[62] In a vicious cycle, it is also a cause as well as effect of the weakening of the father's vital protective and providing role in the family. Whatever we think of the merits of the traditional family structure, the fact is that in the course of a lifetime, we have witnessed the turning upside-down of norms of that family structure and we are now in uncharted water both in family life and as a society.

Drink driving can result in others getting hurt, regardless of the driver's intentions, so for the sake of our own safety and the safety of others, we make plans not to drive even before we start drinking. In the same way, we need to consider all the possible consequences of sex before being sexually active. A couple of decades ago, drink driving was considered by many to be the free choice of the driver. Today, driving while intoxicated is considered to be the height of irresponsibility, but we have a different attitude towards sex outside

---

[62] Abortion statistics, England and Wales: 2019 (publishing.service.gov.uk)

committed marriage. Contraceptives are not 100% effective. The only completely effective method of preventing conception is abstinence, but this is not a choice which is considered valid in today's climate, and will not be until we begin to recognise the humanity of the unborn.

Here, whether we are aware of it or not abortion results from identifying the unborn child with the sin that led to the conception.[63] The same identification happens when a pregnancy results from sexual assault. Even when conception happens within a stable relationship but is just unwanted, the unborn is still made to pay for something out of his or her control, identified with the fact of being an inconvenience.

The fact is that our culture has set the stage for the creation of a large proportion of unwanted pregnancies. This in turn leads to pragmatic arguments.

The common slogan "every child a wanted child" is one which claims to put the welfare of the child first. The supposition is that being unwanted by your parents is worse than death. Abortion is the logical solution to the problem of unwantedness.

We cannot in fact know what the future holds for any of us, let alone a child. We attempt to control our future in various ways, and abortion is certainly a method of control of our circumstances, but life seldom unfolds in the way we imagine.

---

[63] "Sin" is a word rejected by our culture, but it simply means going against the rules which have been set out by God for our own protection.

Some children may be born in apparently auspicious circumstances, but in the end have a challenging childhood. Do we believe that in retrospect they should have been aborted to avoid suffering? Conversely some women may not want the child for emotional or social reasons. These feelings could change over time but abortion leaves no room for a change of heart.

If it is reasonable to determine for the unborn whether their life will be worth living, logically we should be willing for others in turn to decide if our own lives will be worth living too; perhaps once we are old or disabled. If we decide that this denial of autonomy is not reasonable when it comes to our own lives, we must conclude that the unborn should be allowed the same choice about themselves that we demand for ourselves. Since they cannot choose anything at such a young age, we should choose what is best for them until they are old enough to make a decision for themselves. Choosing death for another is taking away from that person all possibility of future choice.

Deciding on behalf of the unborn if their future life will be worth living can be compared to deciding the value of an elderly or disabled person on their behalf: If a person is different from us, and if we consider them to be a burden on society, we are liable to consider their life to be not worth living. In actual fact, this conclusion is rarely come to out of consideration for the welfare of the child, and is usually the result of the weighing up by adults of what is supposed to be best for the adults involved.

Since many adopted children come from a background of unwantedness, abortion as a solution to unwantedness tells adopted children and those in foster care that their lives are not worth living. It is also demonization of foster carers and adoptive parents.

"Every child a wanted child" could be understood in another way. It could be interpreted to mean that we value the life of every child. This may seem unrealistic to us from the perspective of a culture with so many unwanted pregnancies. Yet, if we value the rights of all, not just the most powerful, then we should make room in our culture for all new life, even when they have a disability or if the timing of their arrival is inconvenient.

In the light of the prevalence of this idea, we should also take a good look at the kind of culture which has separated the sexual act from the expectation of procreation. Since conception and pregnancy are such a serious matter, surely we should accommodate this reality, allowing it to be a normal and expected thing that happens mainly when the parents are willing and able to take responsibility for the child. When parents are not willing or able to take responsibility, we should as a culture be willing and able to finance adoption and whatever other actions are necessary for a protected and happy upbringing for the child.

The Redefinition of "Conception"

While reported abortion statistics worldwide are astronomical, the true number is much greater even than this, firstly because of abortions carried out in secret and secondly because of those which women may even be unaware of, through taking contraceptives which can also be abortifacient.

Contraception which only prevents conception (the fertilisation of an egg,) is more likely to fail than a contraception which also thins the lining of the womb, thus preventing implantation of an already conceived embryo. So many contraceptive methods function by preventing ovulation but also by thinning the lining of the womb so that "contraception" is more effective and a greater proportion of unplanned pregnancies are prevented. Parallel to this, over the last few decades there has been a shift in definitions of terms, with the "moment of conception" being separated from the "beginning of pregnancy" (which is described as being the moment of implantation). Thus a method which prevents a fertilised egg which already contains the complete human genome from implanting can still be described as contraception. But this change in definition has been propelled by pragmatism, practicalities of contraception and ideology rather than any biological evidence that life or pregnancy begins at implantation. Some fertilised eggs naturally fail to implant so a pregnancy is more likely to come to full term once implantation has occurred, but to prevent implantation by artificial means is still abortion.

Here are some contraceptive methods which can cause abortion by thinning the lining of the uterus:

1) Emergency Contraception (the "Morning After" Pill, Postcoital Contraception, Plan B, etc.)
2) The Intrauterine Device (IUD)
3) Depo-Provera. This is where hormones are delivered through injections.
4) Oral Contraceptives which contain progesterone only.
5) The Patch (Ortho Evra)
6) The Hormonal Vaginal Contraceptive Ring (NuvaRing)[64]

Scientific advancement

In the same world where abortion is considered to be the solution to an unwanted pregnancy, fertility treatment is offered for those having difficulty in having children.

When people have fertility treatment they can give consent for "spare" embryos to be used in research (up to 14 days of gestation, with the embryo being destroyed afterwards). This has been legal in the UK since 1992, under the justification that at this stage it is a "pre-embryo". But this is an unsubstantiated concept.[65] The human embryo is useful precisely because it is human. Here we see very

---

64
https://abort73.com/abortion_facts/which_birth_control_methods_cause_ab
ortion/
[65] https://www.princeton.edu/~prolife/articles/wdhbb.html

clearly that the embryo is viewed as a commodity. This "altar" could also be described as being that of "having a child."

Another result of the sharp rise in the number of fertility treatments over the last 30 years is the increase in multiple pregnancies (the incidence of twins, triplets etc). In such cases, what is called a "selective termination" is sometimes carried out. This may be considered necessary because "In such cases, the outcome of the pregnancy may be more successful if the number of fetuses is reduced".[66] These selective terminations are carried out at 12 weeks gestation. In 2011, there were 72 selective terminations in England and Wales.[67] By 2019, that yearly total had risen to 126.[68] This is a 75% increase in 9 years. These abortions are carried out under statutory grounds E (substantial risk the child would be born seriously handicapped). But it seems likely that another contributing factor could be that some parents are not prepared to bring up multiple children.

In 2015 the Center for Medical Progress released secretly recorded footage revealing the part played by Planned Parenthood, (the main abortion provider of the USA), in the trafficking of fetal body parts.[69] This has drawn attention to the fact that when an abortion is carried out, parts of the unborn can legally be bought and sold as commodities with the permission of the woman and for the purpose of

---

[66] Abortion statistics, England and Wales: 2019 (publishing.service.gov.uk)
[67] Abortion statistics: England and Wales 2011 - GOV.UK (www.gov.uk)
[68] Abortion statistics, England and Wales: 2019 (publishing.service.gov.uk)
[69] https://en.wikipedia.org/wiki/Planned_Parenthood_2015_undercover_videos_controversy

"scientific advancement." This practice is deemed to be acceptable public policy and is not questioned.[70] In the UK, aborted fetal tissue can be donated for stem cell research, and is considered by some stem cell laboratories as "the right tool for the job," being used for the treatment of some degenerative diseases such as Parkinson's.[71]

This is in no way a new practice. Cells derived from the proceeds of abortion have been exploited in the development of vaccines since as far back as the 1930s, including in the development of the first polio vaccine.[72] This practice continues today since it is effective and because when the woman consents to the exploitation of her unborn, the fetus has no practical legal protections.

Development of at least 5 of the vaccines against Covid-19 has involved use of tissue obtained originally from an aborted unborn. For example the Oxford AstraZeneca vaccine used the HEK-293 cell strain[73] in both development and testing. This is derived from kidney tissue of an apparently healthy female aborted in the Netherlands around 1973,[74] a strain successfully developed after 293 experiments, presumably using the tissue of a number of unborn second trimester fetuses. The Janssen vaccine uses the PER.C6 line which was developed from retinal cells of an 18-week-gestation apparently healthy male aborted in 1985.[75]

---

[70] https://www.ncbi.nlm.nih.gov/books/NBK234204/
[71] https://www.ncbi.nlm.nih.gov/pubmed/18375029
[72] https://edition.cnn.com/2015/07/17/health/fetal-tissue-explainer/index.html
[73] COVID-19 vaccines and aborted fetuses – FactCheckNI
[74] Does AstraZeneca's COVID-19 Vaccine Contain Aborted Fetal Cells? (snopes.com)
[75] Abortion opponents protest COVID-19 vaccines' use of fetal cells | Science | AAAS (sciencemag.org)

To give an idea how many fetuses (of 3 to 6 months' gestation) have been used for the purpose of vaccine development, we may look at the work of the so-called grandfather of modern vaccines, Dr Stanley Plotkin. For a single 1960s study whose purpose was to determine if fetal cells could be used for vaccines, a total of 76 healthy fetuses were used.[76]

Any personal and family information about the unborn whose tissue was used in the making of cell lines has been lost because adults did not see these unborn as having any importance or identity at all. But if we believe what the Bible tells us, we must understand that God knows these individuals intimately. We have seen that He knows each of us from our mother's womb. He knows us not by number but by name.

The regenerative properties of fetal cells have been used in beauty products[77] and there is evidence of illegal trading where women have been paid to have an abortion in order to produce the fetal tissue required for anti-aging jabs.[78] Although there is no proof, it seems probable that these women became pregnant specifically to be able to have an abortion for this purpose. Here we see the unborn being mercilessly exploited in humanity's quest for youth and beauty.

---

[76] Stanley Plotkin, Vaccines Deposition, Under Oath, 9 Hour Full Video - YouTube starting at 7 hours 43 minutes and ending at 7 hours 46 minutes

[77] https://www.washingtontimes.com/news/2009/nov/3/aborted-fetus-cells-used-in-anti-aging-products/

[78] https://www.theguardian.com/world/2005/apr/17/ukraine.russia

"When we consider that women are treated as property, it is degrading to women that we should treat our children as property to be disposed of as we see fit."

These are the words of the nineteenth century feminist leader, Elizabeth Cady Stanton, who lived in a time when a woman's property passed to her husband upon marriage so that her legal identity ceased to exist. The modern-day use, upon the consent of the mother, of aborted and "spare" embryos for research, and ultimately for items such as anti-aging products, demonstrates that we have come to the point of "degrading women" by disposing of our children and using them as commodities to a degree not even imaginable in the time of early feminists, in a way which is so unbelievable to us that perhaps it is easier to shut our eyes to this reality.

More reasons for abortion to be considered

Pressure and Coercion

This could be from someone who has power or authority over the woman such as a boyfriend, husband, or parents of a young mother. (In one US survey, nearly 30% of respondents admitted that they were afraid that they would lose their partner if they failed to terminate their pregnancy.)[79] Women who are being sexually exploited and trafficked are highly likely to undergo one or more forced abortions:

In a series of focus groups conducted around the United States by anti-trafficking activist Laura Lederer in 2014, over 25% of survivors of domestic sex trafficking who responded to the question reported that they had been forced to have an abortion.[80]

This is another area where mainstream media fails to report the scale of an issue which speaks to the lack of "choice" which occurs when abortion is freely available.

Where the mother's life is at risk

Statutory grounds A and F give permission for abortion if continued pregnancy risks the mother's life. This is a difficult scenario but although it is often cited to justify abortion, cases are very rare; so rare indeed that of the more than 200,000 abortions that

---

[79] https://www.pop.org/many-american-women-felt-pressured-abortions-study-finds/

[80] See also: https://www.icmec.org/wp-content/uploads/2015/10/Health-Consequences-of-Sex-Trafficking-and-Implications-for-Identifying-Victims-Lederer.pdf

took place in England and Wales in 2019, only 181 took place on grounds A, B and F[81] combined, with no specific figures for grounds A or F alone.

An example of this situation is if the mother is diagnosed with Cancer while pregnant. Any Cancer treatment designed to save the life of the woman would put the unborn in danger. We know that the unborn relies on the adult woman for life, so saving the mother's life is paramount. But instead of abortion, actions can be taken to protect the woman's life which may or may not cause the unborn to be miscarried. The end result may be the same as abortion, but the *purpose* was not the intentional killing of the unborn. This difference may appear to be semantic, but there is an important moral distinction between someone dying as a result of our efforts to save the life of the one on whom he or she relies for life, and the active and intentional killing of that person. We must also guard from using such a rare reason for abortion as an excuse for its widespread practice for any reason. Good laws rest on principle rather than on exception.

Rape and/or incest

These are both strongly condemned in the Bible (e.g. Leviticus 18.6, Deuteronomy 22.25). They are an often cited reason for abortion but statistically uncommon. Here the innocent unborn, is punished for the sins of a parent. In no other scenario do we consider it reasonable to retaliate against a third party to the crime. Abortion is

---

[81]

https://assets.publishing.service.gov.uk/government/uploads/system/uploads/attachment_data/file/891405/abortion-statistics-commentary-2019.pdf

also a way for abusive adults to dispose of the evidence of abuse of their underage victim.[82]

There is currently in the UK a campaign for a change in the law which would give victim status to those born as a result of rape so they can prosecute the men who raped their mothers.[83] If this campaign is successful, it will mean that the same child who, while unborn might easily be treated in practice as if they were guilty of a crime punishable by death, once born would be treated legally as victim of that same crime. This demonstrates the illogicality of our thinking when it comes to the status of the unborn.

Rather than abortion, a better response to pregnancy caused in these circumstances would be to place the mother in a safe environment and protect her from any future harm. This harm includes further assault through abortion. After such events, victims require extensive counselling and assistance to cope with the negative feeling involved. A rush to abortion as a solution in these circumstances is not helpful to the victim but simply compounds any trauma.

As British law stands, a convicted rapist can under certain circumstances potentially be involved in important decisions affecting their child's upbringing.[84] This means that the victim may continue to be victimized, and this fact is sometimes given as justification for abortion. Yet the more logical action would be to change the unjust

---

[82] https://www.lifesitenews.com/blogs/englands-rotherham-rape-gangs-are-a-perfect-example-of-the-abortion-sex-abu

[83] Why children born of rape must be recognised as victims | Rape and sexual assault | The Guardian

[84] Parental responsibility: is a rapist father still a father? (familylaw.co.uk)

and iniquitous laws around custody so that this right for convicted rapists no longer exists.

Conclusion

We may be able to sympathise more or less with different reasons for abortion, but the bottom line is that these are all modern "altars" upon which the unborn are sacrificed. Or we could describe them as modern-day idols requiring sacrifices. Looking at this list of all-too-common reasons for abortions, who are we to say that women in ancient times did not feel the same necessity to sacrifice their children to Molech that women feel nowadays when it comes to abortion?

Chapter 8: The End Justifies the Means?

In practice, abortion is not an end in itself but rather a means to an end. It is something which for a particular reason is considered necessary to achieve something or to avoid an unwanted situation. Perhaps we can see this reality in clearer definition by looking at what is happening in some other countries.

India has one of the largest populations of the world, with a total of 1.37 billion. It is projected to add another 230 million by 2050. Those who consider population control to be the most important and pressing issue of the country see abortion as a legitimate means to an end of environmental sustainability. The reality is that most abortions are sex-selective, with girls being overwhelmingly aborted. The main reason for this is that girl children are not considered valuable. So in order to prevent the undesired end of having a girl child, women and men have chosen the means of abortion.

It has been estimated that during all the wars combined in the world between 1900 and 1990, the total number of civilians killed was 62 million.[85] But India has lost over 63 million girls in the single decade between 2008 and 2018 due to the widespread practice of sex-selective abortion.[86] Added to this, the practice of killing young baby girls has become routine, and surviving girls in India are subject to many forms of violence. This situation stems from a cultural

---

[85] https://www.nytimes.com/2003/07/06/books/chapters/what-every-person-should-know-about-war.html
[86] https://www.theguardian.com/world/2018/jan/30/more-than-63-million-women-missing-in-india-statistics-show

perception that females are a burden on families and have little or no value. So we see that abortion although seen as a solution, is in fact a symptom of a deeper cultural and spiritual problem of not valuing girls.

In the UK, we may disagree with the aim of not having girl children but if population control is the most important goal and we ignore the effects of disproportionate abortions of girls, then this means that we think this is a reasonable price to pay. We must also recognise that other societies have different values and priorities. If we agree that abortion is a legitimate means to solve a problem, as perceived by the woman, and if we must always trust the grown woman to make the decision on whether to continue with a pregnancy, then the line must not be drawn at any point. Any reason which the woman has for abortion must be considered acceptable. We must in that case consider reasons for abortion such as revenge upon the father, concern to maintain a good figure, concern that pregnancy will prevent the woman from going on holiday and any conceivable reason a woman may have to be totally acceptable and valid.

The most common reasons for abortion in the UK are not sex selection. Perhaps we can consider the situation in India as a parallel to the one in the UK, where our society increasingly views abortion as a solution to a problem, but fails to see that there is a deeper problem which abortion serves only to hide from view. Where there is a perceived need for liberalisation of abortion, this is a symptom of a deeper malaise. Saying that the end justifies the means only masks the reality that the end is itself the result of wrong thinking.

In India there have been some unintended consequences to such widespread sex-selective abortion: In a report, the Special Rapporteur on Contemporary Forms of Slavery for the United Nations warned of unequal numbers of men and women leading to an increase in trafficking of women for forced marriage or surrogacy.[87] This has already been happening in China where the one-child policy has caused a similar situation. Here we see that the result of the widespread cultural decision that the end justifies the means creates more problems, suffering and injustice which will require hard work and investment to attempt to resolve.

An "end" which we may consider to be a legitimate reason for abortion may be the curbing of populations in poor countries. This may or may not be an aim of those countries themselves, but population control has been an increasing concern to governments and society in the West, particularly because of increasing concerns over ecological destruction resulting from population pressures. Abortion is becoming the means by which governments in the developed world wish to achieve the end of lower populations globally.

In many African countries, abortion is currently illegal, culturally alien and stigmatized, but it is presently being pushed as a "right for women" as part of reproductive health services funded by Western developed nations and directed at the developing world. The UK government website tells us that new UK aid support for the Safe

---

[87] https://www.catholicnewsagency.com/news/legal-group-warns-about-sex-selective-abortion-on-day-of-the-girl-child-24320

Abortion Action Fund (SAAF) will "give some of the world's poorest and most vulnerable women and girls access to safe abortion".[88] The UK Department for International Development (DFID) increased its funding of the abortion providing giant, Marie Stopes International (renamed MSI Reproductive Choices), by 5000% between 2006 and 2018. IPAS is a US-based NGO which works to promote sexual and reproductive rights, mainly contraception and abortion. Both MSI and IPAS operate extensively in the developing world.

The justification for this provision of abortion from outside countries is that limiting women's choices increases the number of unwanted pregnancies and increases the practice of unsafe back-street abortions. UK aid will provide £2 million to the SAAF, aiming to "build a world where women's rights to a safe and legal abortion are established and protected".[89]

Western organizations and donors know that most African countries are culturally resistant to abortion, not sharing the aim of making abortion ubiquitous as a means of population control. Governments and NGO's are also aware of the developing world's sensitivities over the idea of a western agenda and laws being imposed on them. They know that if local people were aware of the pressures from the West to impose legalization and unlimited availability of abortion on them, they would sense colonialism and would be strongly opposed to it.

---

[88] https://www.gov.uk/government/news/uk-aid-to-help-prevent-unsafe-abortions
[89] https://www.gov.uk/government/news/uk-aid-to-help-prevent-unsafe-abortions

So as a result, abortion is pushed secretly and illegally in some countries by Western groups for ideological purposes in a way which has been likened to imperialism.[90] DFID has been accused of using millions of pounds of UK tax payers' money to influence developing countries and export abortion. International businesses profit from this, being connected to governments which act according to a hidden abortion agenda. Zambia, for example, has banned the British abortion provider MSI from the country because it committed over 500 illegal abortions there.[91] It was also ordered to "immediately cease and desist offering any form of abortion services in all its facilities within the Republic of Kenya",[92] after complaints that it was promoting abortion in a country where it is illegal unless the woman's life and health are in danger. Niger later ordered the closure of two clinics run by MSI, and the Government threatened to take legal steps against those involved in the promotion of illegal abortions. So we see that MSI has been accused of breaking national laws in at least 3 of the countries where it operates.

The UK Government contributes £140 million to MSI and US-based IPAS[93], which work 'behind the scenes' and 'under the radar' to *deliberately change* Government policies on abortion in South Sudan and Malawi.[94] The UK government has assured British tax

---

[90] https://cmfblog.org.uk/2019/09/26/uk-government-using-strategies-of-concealment-to-hide-its-imposition-of-abortion-on-developing-countries/
[91] https://c-fam.org/turtle_bay/zambia-bans-marie-stopes-for-illegal-abortions/
[92] https://www.reuters.com/article/us-kenya-abortion-rights/kenya-bans-charity-marie-stopes-from-providing-abortion-services-idUSKCN1NO1OM
[93] https://cmfblog.org.uk/2019/09/26/uk-government-using-strategies-of-concealment-to-hide-its-imposition-of-abortion-on-developing-countries/

payers that if any of our tax monies are given for abortion in developing countries, it is used in accordance with the receiving nation's legislation. But there is a clear monetary link between DFID and MSI along with IPAS, with a lack of clarity over what the money is actually being spent on. What can be ascertained is that the UK and other governments are working behind the scenes to influence abortion laws and practice in developing countries. In Malawi and South Sudan, IPAS and MSI are not only partners which assist in provision of these services, but they have also become political participants in processes to shape or reform national policy environments.[95]

Abortion providers like BPAS and MSI have charitable status but make substantial profits from connections to government, so one may wonder the extent to which the forces behind the abortion industry are "pro-choice" and how much they are "pro-profit" and ideology.

We may be concerned in Britain primarily with what happens within our shores, but we must be aware of what is being done by our government with our tax money in our name. Our taxes are currently going towards funding and promoting the practice of abortion in poor countries rather than towards finding imaginative ways to help solve the problems which may cause people to seek out abortion in the first place. It may be culturally acceptable currently in the UK to consider that abortion is a justifiable means to the end of population control, but this is not acceptable in other countries. Even the aim of

---

[94] https://www.tandfonline.com/doi/full/10.1080/17441692.2018.1446545
[95] ibid

population control is not considered important in many countries. Since the bottom half of the world's population collectively own only 1% of the global household wealth[96] we must wonder if the unborn in these poorer countries are perhaps being made to pay the price and scapegoated for the world's inequalities, which are caused by the wealthiest of those who have been born. The surreptitious imposition of abortion on foreign nations by our own must indicate that since the means and method are dishonest, perhaps the end is wrong too.[97]

The idea that "the end justifies the means is not a new one. Let's compare current "end justifies the means" attitudes to abortion, to the concept as it first manifested in the Garden of Eden: In the book of Genesis, Adam and Eve were commanded not to eat of the forbidden fruit, but they ate anyway.[98] Since they did not want to die, why did they choose to eat?

Eve listened to the serpent satan because he gave some good reasons to eat the forbidden fruit. It was "good fruit for getting wisdom, to become like God".[99] This was something she wanted. Eve did not choose to eat because she wanted to die, she ate because she wanted something *good* (wisdom and power). There was a minimisation of the "badness" of the bad action which was required to achieve that "good" thing, and an over-importance of the goodness of the goal. She looked at the goal and considered that the end

---

[96] UNU-WIDER : Blog : The Global Distribution of Household Wealth
[97] For more information on this subject, readers may like to look up the work of Obianuju Ekeocha, the founder and president of Culture of Life Africa, or look up her groundbreaking documentary, "Strings Attached."
[98] **Genesis 2.15-3.6**
[99] **Genesis 3.6**

justified the means. This was the lie, and what led to death. So we can learn from this that if we have to do something bad to achieve something we consider good, then our aim is likely to be wrong. We learn that if we have to compromise truth to achieve what we want, we sacrifice life in the process, and become a perpetrator of darkness. Then we become an agent of the lie, taking part in it and perpetuating it. This is the very essence of the abortion industry.

Individuals are not just the innocent victims of satan; we are complicit in our own downfall. And we can only be deceived because once we cease to love truth we come to value and believe the lie. People are not tempted by an evil which openly calls itself evil. We are tempted by something that we consider to be good but which can only be gained at the cost of doing wrong. We focus on the fruit which we think is good. But God looks at how we got the fruit. So when we think we have to do something bad to achieve something good, we cease to live in God's economy and begin to be in the enemy's scheme. God says that the end cannot justify the means.[100]

Once we agree with the principle that abortion is a legitimate solution to an inconvenient or unplanned pregnancy then we open the door to more and more barbarism and infringement of human rights, since once we fail to protect the right to life, we have destroyed the very reason to protect any rights at all.

Thus we have the situation in the UK where a judge ordered a forced abortion on a woman with learning difficulties, saying that

---

[100] **Romans 3.8:** And why not say (just as we are slanderously reported and as some claim that we say), "Let's do evil that good may come of it"? Their condemnation is deserved.

doctors can physically restrain her to administer the anaesthetic.[101] The reason for such a decision could be that no one is willing to look after the baby once born, but the disabled woman's mother stated her willingness and ability to bring up her grandchild. The idea may be that any child the disabled woman has must automatically be born with a disability (which is not necessarily the case) but if the disabled child must not be allowed to be born then we are saying that the disabled mother should never have been born either. Or the forced abortion may be because the woman's disability means she could not consent to sex so the pregnancy was necessarily caused by rape. Therefore, to undo one wrong, another thing to which she does not consent is done to her; another violence.

So here we have a violation of a disabled person's human rights which is indeed comparable to what was done to people in Nazi Germany. This is just one case where we can see the logical conclusion of considering that the end justifies the means.

We must also consider the probability that increased pressure for abortion on demand will increase the pressure for terminations of other lives which are valuable to God but not necessarily to our society, such as those of the extremely elderly or the terminally sick. We are already seeing this happening today, with the legalisation of euthanasia in a number of European countries, but this will only increase as we ignore the threat to unborn life.

---

[101] https://www.spuc.org.uk/News/ID/384193/UK-woman-who-was-ordered-to-have-a-forced-abortion-in-June-has-given-birth

The answer to a crisis pregnancy is to eliminate the crisis, not the child. Many different circumstances can lead to someone considering abortion. Sometimes those circumstances are very challenging and difficult. But the fact remains that for the unborn to pay the ultimate price for those difficulties is to identify him or her with those problems. If we look carefully at the reason we find ourselves in those challenging circumstances, we will find that at the root, the presence of evil has caused that situation. Abortion comes from equating the unborn with the evil which led to the perceived necessity for abortion. But the good news is that Jesus was identified with all sin in all ages while on the cross, so that there could be forgiveness for all the times we acted upon the principle that "the end justifies the means." (See **chapter 1B, "Restoration"** p.113).

Chapter 9: What's the Damage?

9a: Spiritual Harms to Adults

If we accept that the unborn are human and that they are alive, then we must accept that abortion is nothing short of murder, so the consequences will be the same as any other murder. God's judgement on Cain for murdering Abel was a curse, specifically on the work he put his hand to, which caused him to struggle for survival for the rest of his life.[102] Another effect on the one who sheds innocent blood is the loss of moral compass and a loss of peace.[103]

We saw in **chapter 7a** how God condemned the practice of "passing children through the fire" in an offering to Molech. The location for this sacrifice was also the place where the city's rubbish was burnt. It was called the Valley of Hinnom, or the Valley of Slaughter. An alternative name was Gehenna. In the New Testament, Gehenna signifies hell, the place for eternal burning of the wicked. It is the opposite of life in the Kingdom of God.[104]

---

[102] **Genesis 4.12:** When you cultivate the ground, it will no longer yield its strength to you; you will be a vagrant and a wanderer on the earth.

[103] **Isaiah 59.7-8:** Their feet run to evil, And they hurry to shed innocent blood; Their thoughts are thoughts of wrongdoing, Devastation and destruction are in their paths. They do not know the way of peace, And there is no justice in their tracks; They have made their paths crooked, Whoever walks on them does not know peace.

[104] **Matt 10.28:** And be not afraid of those killing the body, and are not able to kill the soul, but fear rather Him who is able both soul and body to destroy in gehenna. [YLT] **Mark 9.43:** And if thy hand may cause thee to stumble, cut it off. It is better for thee maimed to enter into the life, than having the two hands, to go away to the gehenna, to the fire... [YLT]

So this place was literally a rubbish tip where child sacrifice was carried out, but spiritually it is hell, where the wicked are destroyed. It is a place where the innocent take the place of the wicked and are treated as rubbish, paying the price for the sins of the guilty which are deserving of hell.

The spiritual consequence to women of abortion (and also to the men who facilitate or force it as well as everyone else responsible) is that we begin to struggle for survival ourselves, we lose our peace, and ultimately, we are deserving of hell. This is the bad news. (See **chapter 1B, "Restoration,"** (p.113) for God's solution to this).

**"Abortion has become
The greatest destroyer of peace,
Because it destroys two lives,
The life of the child
And the conscience of the mother."**

(Mother Teresa of Calcutta)

9b: Emotional Harms

Psychological surveys and studies on the subject of harms to women of abortion need to be carefully carried out since it is not always easy to separate the harm caused by the abortion from the damage which led to the person considering the abortion. The studies which receive most publicity are not necessarily the ones with the best methodology but rather the ones which confirm the prevailing assumptions.

Due to this climate, women who have had an abortion can feel under pressure to express relief or to simply keep it a secret. Burying these feelings leads to problems which have become so common that psychologists have coined the term "Post-Abortion Syndrome" (PAS). Symptoms include guilt, anxiety, depression, and thoughts of suicide, drug or alcohol abuse, eating disorders, a desire to avoid children or pregnant women, and flashbacks to the abortion itself. These symptoms are partly due to the absence of validation for the grief and anger which the woman may feel about the abortion:

"We have a saying in the world of therapy. "Secrets kill." Thus is the path of many women after abortion. Don't talk. Don't feel. Keep the secret."[105]

To understand the actual effect of abortion on the emotional wellbeing of women, it is necessary to look at studies which take into account their mental health previous to the abortion. Abortion should

---

[105] Trudy M. Johnson, M.A., LMFT, quoted here: https://www.lifesitenews.com/resources/abortion/abortion-risks/feelings-after-abortion-post-abortion-syndrome

not be considered in isolation, but is usually partly cause and partly effect of other traumas.

A peer-reviewed study published in the International Journal of Environmental Research and Public Health examines the effects of pregnancy loss (including abortion) on mental health specifically in the six months after previously mentally healthy women have given birth to a subsequent child.

It was found that induced abortion or miscarriage of a first pregnancy increases the risk of mental health problems within 6 months of the birth of a subsequent child by 10 to 35 percent. There was also an 83 percent increase in risk that those mental health problems would lead to hospitalization. This study confirms that having an abortion may exacerbate pre-existing psychiatric problems, but may also mark the onset of problems that did not previously exist.

Here we have evidence that unresolved memories and feelings about pregnancy loss need to be dealt with, otherwise they can lead to post-natal depression and even psychosis during a subsequent pregnancy.

When these feelings are not validated and worked through, women may take to alcohol and drugs to numb those negative feelings. Others enter a life of promiscuity and repeat abortions, trapped in the vicious cycle of abandonment and rejection. They may suffer eating disorders, panic attacks, depression, anxiety, and thoughts of suicide.[106]

---

[106] https://www.mdpi.com/1660-4601/18/4/2179

Other robust studies have found the following:

1) Previously mentally healthy women, who have an abortion, experience nearly twice the level of mental health problems as those who have not had an abortion.

2) This group of women also have three times the risk of major depressive illness compared to the other groups.[107]

3) Women who have had an abortion are significantly more likely to be admitted to hospital (both single and recurrent admissions) for psychiatric problems including depression and bipolar disorder.[108]

4) Studies have found that women who have had an abortion are at significantly higher risk of PTSD even up to 10 years after the event.[109]

5) Women who have had an abortion are more likely to suffer from depression and anxiety in the medium to long term than those who have had a miscarriage.[110]

---

[107] https://www.cmf.org.uk/resources/publications/content/?context=article&id=1850

[108] Reardon DC et al. Can Med Assoc J 2003; 168:1253-5 found here: https://www.ncbi.nlm.nih.gov/pmc/articles/PMC1188167/

[109] https://www.cmf.org.uk/resources/publications/content/?context=article&id=1850

[110] Broen AN et al. Acta Obstet Gynecal Scand 2006; 85:317-23, quoted here: https://www.cmf.org.uk/resources/publications/content/?context=article&id=1850

6) Women have a higher risk of suffering psychological trauma after abortion if they feel it was forced by others or by circumstances.[111]

Another risk factor is if the abortion is a medical or chemical one (The RU-486 drug). In 2019, 73% of abortions in the UK were medically induced.[112] The trend is towards more medically induced abortion. This method has become the norm during the Covid-19 pandemic since women have (so far) temporarily been permitted to obtain the abortion pill on the strength of a face time consultation only. At the time of writing, there is pressure for that temporary relaxation of the regulations to be made permanent, so that women will continue to be able to obtain the abortion pill without the usual health and safeguarding checks such as making sure that the pregnancy is not above the 10 week gestation limit for medical abortion, or that it is not an ectopic pregnancy (which requires medical assistance). This must be concerning, not just on the level of physical safety, but also since it means that the woman may actually see the remains of her baby and have to dispose of them in whichever way she can. It means that the most traumatic and medically challenging events occur when the woman is probably alone and in great physical pain.[113]

---

[111] Priscilla Coleman, Abortion and mental health: quantitative synthesis and analysis of research published 1995–2009 (2011) quoted here: http://bjp.rcpsych.org/content/199/3/180

[112] Abortion statistics, England and Wales: 2019 (publishing.service.gov.uk)

[113] https://www.lifesitenews.com/resources/abortion/abortion-risks/feelings-after-abortion-post-abortion-syndrome

Harms to Men

In a discussion of emotional harm caused to the adults involved in abortion, the fathers involved are often forgotten. Although this has not been studied to a fraction of the detail of women's experience, there is unquestionably harm done.[114] The decision to have an abortion rests with the woman and her doctors alone.[115] Legally the father of the unborn, whether he is the woman's husband or not, has no right to demand or refuse an abortion. Abusive partners can put pressure on women to have an abortion, but also loving partners and husbands who want to have the child, may discover that their wishes are considered irrelevant by government and society. The main harm done to men has thus been found to be due to feelings of helplessness, together with guilt, grief and loss. Typically, in men this can lead to depression, anxiety, or the urge to be compulsive, controlling, demanding and directing. Or they can become enraged. Abortion may be seen as the only option due to an already unstable relationship, but cause and effect can be difficult to unravel. The emotional harm to men may be one of the reasons that relationships overwhelmingly do not survive after abortion.

---

[114] The Effects of Abortion on Men: its Emotional, Psychological and Relational Impact by Vincent M. Rue, Cynthia Tellefsen, found here: https://www.catholicculture.org/culture/library/view.cfm?id=8089
[115] https://www.rcog.org.uk/globalassets/documents/guidelines/abortion-guideline_web_1.pdf

Much has been studied and written about emotional consequences of abortion, and this has been just a quick over-view, so for those interested in this topic, further reading is recommended.[116]

**One life taken, many
hearts broken**

---

[116] For more information on post-abortion PTSD and psychological harms: https://herchoicetoheal.com/

9c: Physical Harms to Women

Again, there is much controversy surrounding this research area due to our current political, social and spiritual climate, but abortion without harm to the woman is impossible.

One of the major effects of abortion on the woman's body is caused by **Fetal microchimerism.** Fetal cells are transferred by fetal-maternal hemorrhage, (bleeding from the placenta being destroyed during abortion). The unborn's blood mingles with the mother's. These cells persist in the woman's body long-term[117] and may become embedded in maternal organs like the heart, liver, brain, thyroid etc.

There are higher concentrations of fetal cells in the maternal circulation after abortion than after miscarriage. There are also higher rates after surgical abortion than after medical abortions.[118] Fetal microchimeric cells have been found in brain and nervous system tumours and cells of fetal origin have been detected in various cancers including **thyroid, breast cervix, lung** and **melanoma**.

Fetal microchimerism has an association with diseases like **systemic sclerosis, system lupus erythematosus, primary biliary cirrhosis, autoimmune thyroid diseases** and **juvenile myositis.**[119,120]

---

[117] https://www.ncbi.nlm.nih.gov/pmc/articles/PMC3921195/

[118] https://creation.com/how-abortion-harms-women, quoting: Peterson, S.E., Nelson, J.L., Guthrie, K.A., Gadi, V.K., Aydelotte, T.M., Oyer, D.J., Prager, S.W., and Gammill, H.S., Prospective assessment of fetal-maternal cell transfer in miscarriage and pregnancy termination, *Hum. Reprod.* **27**(9):2607–2612, 2012 | doi: 10.1093/humrep/des244

[119] Sarkar, K. and Miller, F.W., Possible roles and determinants of microchimerism in autoimmune and other disorders, *Autoimmun. Rev.*

Abortion risks long term health problems such as **autoimmune diseases, infertility, ectopic pregnancy** and **Cancer**.

Breast Cancer:

The connection between abortion and breast Cancer is disputed. The Royal College of Obstetricians and Gynaecologists has stated that: 'Women should be informed that induced abortion is not associated with an increase in breast cancer risk'.[121] We have medical articles which state that: 'There is no evidence of an association between abortion and breast cancer.'[122] These papers are commonly cited to dismiss any evidence of a link. Cancer Research UK has also stated that abortion does not increase the chance of developing breast cancer.

But this is not a settled matter. There are many risk factors for breast Cancer. Most factors are related to reproduction and/or female reproductive hormones. The more children a woman has, and the younger she is when she has the first, the less likely she is to contract breast Cancer in her lifetime. Breast feeding is also protective against this form of Cancer. Childlessness, use of hormonal contraceptives, use of Hormone replacements (HRT) and induced abortion are all

3(6):454–463, 2004 found here:
https://www.ncbi.nlm.nih.gov/pubmed/15351311
[120] Chauhan, V., Thakur, A., Sharma, G., Abortion may be associated with elevated risk of future hypothyroidism. *Int J Crit Illn Inj Sci.* **8**(1):41-43, 2018. doi: 10.4103/IJCIIS.IJCIIS_43_17found here:
https://www.ncbi.nlm.nih.gov/pmc/articles/PMC5869800/
[121] https://www.rcog.org.uk/globalassets/documents/guidelines/abortion-guideline_web_1.pdf
[122] (PDF) Misinformation on abortion (researchgate.net)

conducive towards breast Cancer. The evidence for this is still contested since surveys need to isolate each contributing factor, but there is now significant literature to support this.

Hormonal contraceptives and abortions can act in combination. Abortion stops a process which was in full flow, leaving breast cells in a state of interrupted development making them more likely to become cancerous. The estrogen in the hormonal contraceptives helps to develop the cancer.[123]

We have seen a steep rise in breast cancer cases in the West in the last decades. In the UK since the early 1990s, breast cancer incidence has increased by nearly a quarter.[124] The introduction of screening can account for an initial rise in rates but does not account for the continued rise in rates of new cases after screening has been in force for several years. Of key importance is that more women with the experience of abortion and use of hormonal contraceptives have entered the age group now being screened.[125]

In a major study, a meta analysis of 14 provinces in China, it was found that one abortion increases the risk of breast Cancer by 44%, with the risk of contracting Cancer later in life increasing with each additional abortion.[126]

Each additional abortion increases the risk of disease, a fact that is becoming more significant. Abortion is becoming progressively more

---

[123] https://www.jpands.org/vol22no1/carroll.pdf
[124] UK Breast Cancer Statistics | Breast Cancer UK
[125] https://www.jpands.org/vol22no1/carroll.pdf
[126] A study published in the prestigious medical journal Fetal Causes Control, sited in https://lifecharity.org.uk/news-and-views/major-chinese-study-shows-significant-abortion-breast-cancer-link/

normalized in British culture with more women having multiple abortions. Data revealed under the Freedom of Information Act from the Department of Health for England and Wales and NHS Scotland has revealed that in 2018:

Over 80 thousand repeat abortions were carried out, with nearly 3 and a half thousand of these being carried out on teenagers. The year-on-year trend is for more multiple abortions. In the same year 718 women had their 6th abortion. 5 of these women were still teenagers.[127] One wonders how many abortions this group of teens will have had by the end of their lives, and how much increased risk of contracting the various illnesses associated. One may also wonder if these girls and women were able to give consent which was informed, having been advised of the risks associated especially with multiple terminations.

---

[127]https://news.sky.com/story/abortions-five-teenagers-among-women-who-had-at-least-their-6th-termination-in-uk-last-year-11863920

The "Do No Harm" Medical Principle

So why is there such resistance to an admission that the widespread practice of abortion is one contributing factor to the rise in cases of breast Cancer as well as many other diseases? One of the reasons is that in the UK, at the time of writing, every abortion requires the signatures of 2 doctors under the 1967 Abortion Act. Most medical professional liability insurance claims are made in the area of obstetrics and gynecology. So if women who experienced breast cancer could make medical claims against the doctors who signed off their abortion, then there could be an avalanche of claims, as has been the case in the tobacco industry regarding lung cancer. In this light, it is easy to understand why British medical journals are reluctant to publish papers which report a link between abortion and breast cancer, and promote papers which report the absence of a link.[128] This may also be one reason that politicians and pressure groups are pushing for complete legalization of abortion up to birth, meaning that they can be carried out on any premises, and without the signature of any doctor. Thus there can be no legal liability.

In the broader context, there may be a number of factors which may explain why harms of abortion to women are generally not taken into consideration. Our culture is built upon the concept of the kind of freedom of which contraception and abortion have become emblematic. To point out problems with them can be seen as an attack

---

[128] A study published in the prestigious medical journal Fetal Causes Control, sited in https://lifecharity.org.uk/news-and-views/major-chinese-study-shows-significant-abortion-breast-cancer-link/

on freedom or on women. The reality is quite the opposite, however. The only true consent for a medical procedure is informed consent.ff

Conclusion

In addition to killing the unborn, abortion harms women physically in ways which they are not warned by abortion providers, harms which continue for years afterwards. Since medical training is based on the principle of "do no harm," practitioners involved in abortion need to re-consider the ethical basis on which they operate. The link seems almost as clear as the link between tobacco smoking and lung cancer, and we see the same vested interests in the multi-million pound abortion industry. It is no wonder that the real risk of great physical harms is not part of pre-abortion counseling, thus women's consent for abortion is not generally informed consent.

The physical damage done to women through abortion is a picture and consequence of the spiritual damage done, and evidence that the Word of God is true and reliable. Ignorance of the commands of God does not protect us from the consequences of going against them. See the next chapter, (**1B, "Restoration"**) for the antidote.

Chapter 1B: Restoration

We have seen **in chapter 1A** that there is no limit to the power of God's grace to save. Then we enumerated the many different levels on which abortion destroys those involved. Let's look at the specific consequences from which we can be forgiven.

Although God deals with the sin of abortion in the same way as any other sin, there is a difference in significance since this is murder, and the victim is entirely innocent. The blood of the innocent unborn can only be redeemed by the shedding of the innocent blood of the Son of God. When there is a murder of an innocent, his or her blood speaks and demands justice. This is what causes the curse. The only freedom from that curse is the blood of another innocent, the perfect One, Jesus, who exchanged His life for that of the innocent child, and his life for ours once and for all. This is the essence of the exchange which takes place at the cross.[129]

If we know this, but still doubt that it is possible for this particular sin to be forgiven, then we must consider that either the God who said this has made complete provision for our *complete* salvation, and *complete* healing... or He is a liar.

Those who think that their sin is too bad to be forgiven, must consider what the exchange at the Cross means. It means that the

---

[129] **Genesis 4.10-11:** [God] said, "What have you done? The voice of your brother's blood is crying to Me from the ground. Now you are cursed from the ground, which has opened its mouth to receive your brother's blood from your hand.. **Hebrews 12.24: ...**and to Jesus, the mediator of a new covenant, and to the sprinkled blood, which speaks better than the blood of Abel.

abundance of grace and power contained in Jesus, is available to each one of us, and is more than enough to pay for not just the worst sin, but multiplied by billions of people across the world and down the centuries. This is true abundance. He has made it possible for anyone to obtain forgiveness regardless of their background.[130]

The pro-choice slogan is "my body, my choice". We have seen that abortion entails not just the woman's body but also another person's. But added to this, the Bible tells us that our body is not our own because it was bought at a price by another body. [131]

Thus the pro-choice argument is in direct defiance of God, a choice not only against the physical life of the unborn, but our own eternal life.

Abortion is partly a sin against our own body, as is sexual sin.[132] This is an often-ignored reason that it leads specifically to shame. Abortion itself is often felt as a violent assault on the woman's body, sometimes equated with rape (especially when that abortion is forced or coerced). But Christ died in His *body*, not just symbolically. He physically took on a body, and took our sins and sicknesses in His Body, including those sins which we take into our body. He took our shame and died a shameful death. Then He rose again in His *body*,

---

[130] **2 Peter 3.9:** The Lord is not slow about His promise, as some count slowness, but is patient toward you, not wishing for any to perish but for all to come to repentance.

[131] **Mark 14.22:** While they were eating, He took some bread, and after a blessing He broke it, and gave it to them, and said, "Take it; this is My body." (See also **Matt 26.26** and **Luke 22.19)**

[132] **1 Corinthians 6.18**

not just as a celestial being. In this way He took our place.[133] The result is an exchange of our shame for His honour.[134]

We have access not only to spiritual salvation but also physical healing in our bodies if we can but grasp this in our understanding and believe that it belongs legally to us who have made this exchange at the Cross. We celebrate this every time we take Holy Communion, recalling Jesus' words, that "this is my body, broken for you." Hence we can be healed from the physical consequences as well as the spiritual and emotional ones enumerated in **chapter 9** of this book. This truly is "good news."

But even this is not the end of the matter! I can know that:

"I have been crucified with Christ;
and it is no longer I who live, but Christ lives in me;
and the life which I now live in the flesh
I live by faith in the Son of God,
who loved me and gave Himself up for me."
(Galatians 2.20)

Thus my body is not my own. We may consider this to be a limitation, but it is in fact liberation.

---

[133] **Isaiah 53.5:** But He was pierced for our offenses, He was crushed for our wrongdoings; The punishment for our well-being was laid upon Him, And by His wounds we are healed.

[134] **Isaiah 61.7:** Instead of your shame you will have a double portion, and instead of humiliation they will shout for joy over their portion. Therefore they will possess a double portion in their land, everlasting joy will be theirs.

The result of repentance and trusting in God for the forgiveness of all sin (including abortion), through Jesus Christ is a legal done-deal. The repentant Christian has a legal right to freedom from the curse resulting from that sin, and to the joy and peace that come from knowing that "it is finished" and paid for in full.

King David of Israel committed sexual sin and then to cover it up and achieve his personal goal, he became morally responsible for the death of the innocent husband of Bathsheba **(2 Samuel 11).** As a direct consequence of this, his own newborn (and also innocent) child died. There were horrible consequences to his actions, yet even this was not an unforgiveable sin. Referring to these events he said:

"Purify me with hyssop, and I will be clean;
Cleanse me, and I will be whiter than snow."
(Psalm 51.7)

He believed in God's forgiveness immediately upon repentance, even for the worst, most shameful sin. He had to live with the consequences of his actions, but he knew that he was forgiven so he could move on from that event. If this was true for David under the Old Covenant, how much more must it be true for us under the New Covenant now?

It is common for women who have had an abortion to keep this a secret, sometimes for decades. Key to being set free from the power of this sin is being able to talk about it to a trusted friend or counsellor and to externalise the negative feelings involved. We are told by many women that there is freedom in the telling.

There will almost certainly be a need to forgive others, particularly when the circumstances of the abortion involved the person being sinned against. This could be in cases of rape or abuse, or if the abortion was coerced, or if financial or emotional support were expected but withheld. Forgiveness does not mean saying that what was done was "okay," it means that we let go of the anger and resentment and trust God to give justice. It is a decision to be taken, not a feeling that we might have. It also does not mean going back into a dangerous and harmful situation.

Then we must forgive ourselves. We receive forgiveness from our Father once and for all but the tendency is to continue to blame ourselves long after we have been forgiven. It is vital to stop punishing ourselves for past actions after we have repented and received forgiveness from God, and to stop accepting false feelings of shame. We must accept forgiveness once and for all because His plan is to take us *beyond* forgiveness to restoration.

Forgiveness is a major topic in itself, and one which there is not space to go into in any more detail here.

Up to now, we have found that the unborn are entirely human and entirely alive from the moment of conception. We conclude from this that destroying that life must be called nothing less than murder. This is not an emotional statement but simply the application of logic. We must call it what it is. And murder carries consequences. In chapter 9, we saw some of the consequences of abortion to the woman physically, emotionally and spiritually. These are all evidence of a curse resulting from the action. Consequently, there must of necessity be a need for deliverance on the part of any woman who has had an abortion, as well as all those involved with it such as abortion practitioners and family members who may have applied pressure for the woman to have the abortion. This is another huge subject which there isn't space to go into detail here, but this is a matter which must be broached by those trying to assist women to deal with the aftermath. Of course, if conception occurred through rape, incest or other traumatic circumstances, deliverance from the effects of these events will also be needed.[135] This cannot be done alone so counselling, prayer and support will be required.

Along with this, we must rest on the truth of what God *says*: His plans are for our prosperity, hope and future.[136]

We are to be content with His plan, not trying to forge our own, but trusting that He wants what is best for us.[137] We are to trust that the work He started through that exchange at the cross, He will complete by His power.[138] So even when our feelings tell us to give up, we know that One stronger than us *is* our strength.

---

[135] I realise that some readers may not be familiar with this idea, but for those who want to get started in this area, read "Blessing or Curse: You Can Choose" by Derek Prince, especially chapter 7.

[136] I know the plans that I have for you,' declares the LORD, 'plans for welfare and not for calamity to give you a future and a hope. (**Jeremiah 29.11**)

[137] **Hebrews 13.5:** Make sure that your character is free from the love of money, being content with what you have; for He Himself has said, "I WILL NEVER DESERT YOU, NOR WILL I EVER ABANDON YOU,"

[138] **Philippians 1.6:** For I am confident of this very thing, that He who began a good work among you will complete it by the day of Christ Jesus.

Crucially, we must consider Psalm 139 not just with regard to the unborn, but to ourselves. We must begin to consider not just the unborn but ourselves too to be fearfully and wonderfully made and an awesome part of creation.

As we have seen, the Good News of the Gospel is founded on the concept that all human beings are made in the image of God. But let's pause and consider this properly for a moment. The original foundational truth that we are all made in the image of God can become nothing more than a theological detail to argue over. But in reality if we could only allow this idea to sink into our understanding and really *believe* it, our sense of self-worth as well as our respect for others would be completely revolutionised.

The God of the Bible assures us that regardless of any perceived flaws, regardless of what we have done or not done, regardless of who we are and what we are like *now*, we each have a God-given eternal identity. The realization that abortion is a terrible sin must be followed by the equal and complementary realization that the Lord's purpose and dealings with us are contrastingly magnificent. Since abortion is the product of satan's lie about our identity and eternal destiny, then let's look in the opposite direction to the truth of who we really are. Abortion is like the smoke rising up from the battle, but there's something important to see beyond the smoke, which the lie has been hiding from our view, and it has to do with who we are.

We are also bought at the highest price possible. This must cause us to have the self-respect, dignity and care for ourselves that leads us to respect and care for others. A central theme of the Bible is the paradox of our intrinsic worth because we have been made in the image of God, and our unworthiness because of our sinfulness. This paradox is resolved once and for all at the Cross.[139]

All believers are accused day and night before the Throne of God. But God says that the Accuser is defeated by 3 things:

The work of Jesus on the Cross to pay the legal penalty for sin:

Without this, we would have no defense against any accusation, because there's no getting around sin. Regarding abortion specifically, there can be no forgiveness for this without the powerful actual event of Christ's sacrifice. But conversely, such a serious matter as abortion is a tiny thing when compared to the power of grace available through the "blood of the Lamb." This is activated through repentance upon salvation, but sometimes we need to repent specifically. Due to its seriousness, abortion is one sin which requires specific repentance.

---

[139] **Revelation 12.11:** "And they overcame him [the accuser of the brethren] because of the blood of the Lamb and because of the word of their testimony and they did not love their life even when faced with death."

The word of our testimony:

Once we have received forgiveness we can speak about it without fear of condemnation. We go from the state of being accused and condemned by the Enemy of Christ, to being able to fight back, condemning the one who accuses.[140]

Self-sacrifice:

Rather than literally laying down our lives, at least at the moment in the West, this usually means speaking out and acting in accordance with what we know from God, all in the knowledge that it may be against our interests. Speaking out in defence of the unborn in today's atmosphere is not popular, and it may cause problems at work and socially as well as in the family. We must know, though, that we are not alone when we do this since we have the Lord's promise to be with us when we step out according to His Word.[141]

Those who have been forgiven and restored from the effects of abortion are the best message-bearers because you cannot be accused of not understanding, or of condemning, and you can be like a light-bearer in the darkness for those following behind. This must be the worst and most devastating defeat for satan, to see that all he meant for your destruction has only been used for the salvation of many through you. The stick that was meant to beat you becomes the stick *you* use to beat the enemy.

[140] **Isaiah 54.17:** No weapon that is formed against you will succeed; And you will condemn every tongue that accuses you in judgment. This is the heritage of the servants of the LORD, And their vindication is from Me," declares the LORD.
[141] **1 Samuel 2.30:** ... for those who honor Me I will honor...

> Two wonders here that I confess
> My worth and my unworthiness
> My value fixed, my random paid
> At the Cross.[142]

---

[142] From "My Worth Is Not In What I Own" By Keith Getty

Chapter 10: A National Issue

10a: Effect on a Nation

**If you were a British Tommy (infantry)
in the trenches in World War 1,
you had a 10% chance of being killed.
If you are a baby in the womb today,
you have a 24% chance of being aborted.**

The main function of government, according to Romans 13, is to protect the good and punish the guilty. Since we have established that abortion is the murder of innocents, it must be the function of government to prohibit this and protect the unborn.

One of the main reasons we have laws is to protect the innocent against others. We have laws that prohibit smoking in certain places, to protect those who do not smoke from the harmful effects of the choice of others to smoke. This is because we recognise that the "my body my choice" slogan is no longer valid once my choices affect the body of another human being who has not made that choice. Cigarette packets even contain warnings that smoking may harm the unborn. So our culture already accepts that freedom of choice must be limited where it damages others, even the unborn. But we have chosen to exclude the *unwanted* unborn.

Where a nation does not protect its innocent unborn by law, it cannot prosper. We also have to consider the fact that many women do not want to have an abortion but are forced by people or circumstance into feeling that they have no option. Abortion then becomes an assault on the woman, so here the government and wider society fails in its responsibility to protect women as well as the unborn.

In Britain, we are particularly and peculiarly attached to our National Health Service, which has been a symbol of how the nation cares for its people at their weakest moment. The overwhelming majority of abortions are financed and carried out by the NHS in the name of "essential health care for women," But we have seen that abortion is far from health care for the unborn. Even for women it is damaging on every level. The "do no harm" principle is totally ignored when it comes to abortion. Individual care workers are responsible for their own actions, and in the face of the extent of bloodshed, we cannot expect the NHS as a whole to prosper.

Let's consider an extreme negative example of the state failing monumentally in its responsibility towards its most vulnerable members; in fact it turned against them, actively going out to destroy its own: The Nazi state. The regime sent those of its own people who did not match up to expectation in some way (chiefly German Jews), to a life of fear and degradation, then death in extermination camps. Incidentally, the way this was achieved was first by dehumanising those people and encouraging prejudice against them. This is a principle which was used to justify slavery and is presently being used to justify abortion.

Back to our Nazi analogy: The first thing that was done upon people's arrival in any death camp, was the sorting out of useful labourers on one side from the useless on the other, (it was a very rational system). The useless were marked for the gas chamber, the elderly and sick being in this group as well as the very young.

Under these circumstances, many mothers would make the rational decision to give their baby to an older woman so that both "useless" people would be killed but the young woman had a chance of survival. If they did not do this, then both the mother and child would definitely die. As it was, at least the woman might escape death.

Who of us can judge a mother who did this in such circumstances? It was the most awful dilemma to be faced with.

Let me state the obvious here: they should not have been in that situation in the first place! At the point where the terrible decision was made, the situation was already totally wrong. Thus in fact *no decision* taken at that point could ever be the "right" one.

So taking this as our model, the most important function of government regarding this subject must be to get women to a place where the idea of having an abortion never enters their head as being a reasonable "solution" to a problem; a place where abortion is never thought to be the *only* possibility; a place where they can imagine their child having a life and a future, and where that life is possible and practical. So instead of encouraging abortion as a solution to social and economic problems, good governments focus on dealing with the causes of these problems. These causes would include poverty, poor housing, career ambitions or opportunities, having a wrong sexual partner, rape etc. Bad government has only quick fix measures; good government has a moral compass and cares for the most vulnerable in our society.

Free choice is a basic human right Biblically. Since Western societies are still founded on Judeo-Christian principles they operate according to this concept. But abortion is contrary to this foundational principle because it puts the free choice of adult women before the basic human right to life of the youngest and most vulnerable of society.

Bio-Ethicist and philosopher Peter Singer is among those who reject the idea that government should protect the unborn for reasons based on a religious world-view. The argument is that restricting abortion due to Judeo-Christian principles imposes religion on a whole community of people who may not follow that religion. This idea presupposes that "religion" is a private matter, not connected to real life, but Christianity compels the believer to defend the defenceless.

The Bible says that stealing is wrong. We tend to think of this idea as being common sense but the only requirement for justification of stealing is the redefinition of a word, "theft" being referred to as "redistribution of wealth" etc.

To follow Singer's logic we should say that laws that prohibit stealing are an example of the imposition of religion on unbelievers, but prohibition of theft is an example of how Biblical law is in fact for the benefit of all society, to prevent injustice. So we would do well not to take for granted the influence of Judeo-Christian thought on our legal system, which has been a limiting influence on the abuse of the vulnerable which is natural to man when left to his own devices. Whether a person believes in God or not, the consequences to the person and the nation of ungodly laws will be the same, and although women must take responsibility for their actions in having an abortion, they are the last decision-makers in a long line starting with government, media and opinion-leaders, which set out the framework of thinking which influences decisions made by individuals. Freedom of religion does not allow infringement of someone's rights by another; rather it should protect the rights of the most vulnerable and ultimately benefit us all.

Added to this, all laws come from a section of society's perception of morality, and those laws are always imposed on the section who disagrees.

The prophet Isaiah tells us how the Lord responds to nations who practice injustice and who do not protect their most vulnerable members.[143] Here we see the downward spiral which occurs once a nation rejects God. This rejection leads us to lose track of the essential value of human beings who are created in the image of God. As a result we become wise in our own eyes and begin to see evil as good and good as evil.

When abortion is described as essential health care and a woman's right; when the unborn are described as being a blob of cells who feel no pain or worse: parasites;[144] when the defense of the unborn is

---

[143] **Isaiah 5.20-21:** Woe to those who call evil good, and good evil; Who substitute darkness for light and light for darkness; Who substitute bitter for sweet and sweet for bitter! Woe to those who are wise in their own eyes and clever in their own sight!

[144] Warren Hern, one of the world's most prominent abortionists, wrote that

routinely described as being an expression of judgemental hatred towards women; this is when we know that we are living in a culture which calls evil good and good evil. The Bible tells us that a fearful judgement awaits such a nation.

As we have seen, the Scriptures tell us that firstly, individuals were affected by the shedding of innocent blood. But then whole cities were affected.[145] Next, the whole of the nation was affected because of the relationship between the shedding of innocent blood and the occupying of the land allotted to the nation.[146] The people of Judah were promised that if they did not follow the practices of the Canaanites (chief among them being child sacrifice) then they would be able to flourish in the land.[147] Otherwise they would not prosper, and would ultimately be defeated.[148]

"the relationship between the [mother] and the [baby] can be understood best as one of host and parasite." Warren M. Hern, *Abortion practice* (Philadelphia: J.B. Lippincott Company, 1990), 14

[145] **Jeremiah 26.15:** … if you put me to death, you will bring innocent blood on yourselves, and on this city and on its inhabitants; for truly the LORD has sent me to you to speak all these words in your hearing.

[146] **Deuteronomy 19.10:** So innocent blood will not be shed in the midst of your land which the LORD your God gives you as an inheritance and bloodguiltiness be on you.

[147] **Jeremiah 7.6-7:** …if you do not oppress the stranger, the orphan, or the widow, and do not shed innocent blood in this place, nor follow other gods to your own ruin, then I will let you live in this place, in the land that I gave to your fathers forever and ever..

[148] **Jeremiah 19.4-8:** Since they have abandoned Me … and since they have filled this place with the blood of the innocent and have built the high places of Baal to burn their sons in the fire as burnt offerings …
I will frustrate the planning of Judah and Jerusalem in this place, and I will make them fall by the sword before their enemies and by the hand of those who seek their life; and I will make their carcasses food for the birds of the sky and the animals of the earth. I will also turn this city into an object

The land was defiled by innocent blood so that it did not enjoy the creation blessing of a prosperous nature. Judgement for shedding innocent blood was devastation of the land.[149]

Psalm 106:34-41 gives a succinct explanation of the compromise and tolerance leading first to occult practices and child sacrifice, and ultimately to the devastation of the land and being conquered by other nations:

> *... they got involved with the nations*
> *And learned their practices, And served their idols,*
> *Which became a snare to them.*
> *They even sacrificed their sons and their daughters*
> *to the demons, And shed innocent blood,*
> *The blood of their sons and their daughters*
> *Whom they sacrificed to the idols of Canaan;*
> *And the land was defiled with the blood.*
> *So they became unclean in their practices,*
> *And were unfaithful in their deeds.*
> *Therefore the anger of the LORD*
> *was kindled against His people,*
> *And He loathed His inheritance.*
> *So He handed them over to the nations,*
> *And those who hated them ruled over them.*

of horror and hissing...

[149] **Joel 3.19:** Egypt will become a wasteland, And Edom will become a desolate wilderness, Because of the violence done to the sons of Judah, In whose land they have shed innocent blood..

The shedding of innocent blood is linked to idolatry.[150] A Molech-worshipping nation was judged because it practiced the murder of innocents by forcible, violent abortion for the purpose of gaining power and wealth.[151]

The difficulties which the Israelites encountered from the enemies around them were not the result of military or political issues but moral flaws, chiefly from the shedding of innocent blood in child sacrifice.

God's view of Israel was of a unique nation, so we cannot extrapolate too much from their situation to that of modern nations. But God's perspective on justice never changes. If child sacrifice was an abomination which brought a curse to the whole nation thousands of years ago, then it must receive the same judgement in modern Britain. So if we see a multitude of painful problems in our society today, we would do well to look beyond the obvious social, political and economic triggers to a deeper moral flaw, chiefly the shedding of innocent blood in widespread acceptance and government-sponsored promotion of abortion.

---

[150] **Jeremiah 19.4:** Since they have abandoned Me and have made this place foreign and have burned sacrifices in it to other gods that neither they nor their forefathersnor the kings of Judah had ever known,
and since they have filled this place
with the blood of the innocent

[151] **Jeremiah 22.17:** "But your eyes and your heart are intent only upon your own dishonest gain, and on shedding innocent blood and on practicing oppression and extortion". **Amos 1.13:** This is what the LORD says: "For three offenses of the sons of Ammon, and for four I will not revoke its punishment, Because they ripped open the pregnant women of Gilead in order to enlarge their borders.

Although abortions were carried out before the 1967 Abortion Act, what has changed since then is that it has become Government-approved and financed ultimately by all of us through taxation. In 2018, 98% of abortions were funded by the NHS, and by taxpayer money.[152] Free availability, as well as social changes have led in turn to an exponential increase in the abortion rate: The proportion of UK pregnancies which end in abortion has risen from 2.8 percent in 1967 to 23 percent in 2019.[153]

Since we know from our Biblical model that the murder of innocents leads to all manner of social, economic and political woes, including ultimately a loss of national autonomy, we must therefore conclude that if God's treatment of nations is consistent then the UK should have experienced an equivalent downward spiral since 1967.

On January 1st 1973, the UK's membership of the Common Market came into effect. This eventually became the EU, whose laws eventually superseded UK laws in authority. Perhaps our withdrawal from the EU indicates that we have been given another opportunity to turn the UK's downward spiral into an upward one where the unborn are cherished and we come out from under the heavy hand of judgement of God. But this requires widespread repentance.

Once we open the door to intentional killing, there is no logical stopping point, so we must also consider increasing acceptance of abortion as a catalyst for other challenges to the notion of the sanctity

---

[152]

https://assets.publishing.service.gov.uk/government/uploads/system/uploads/attachment_data/file/808556/Abortion_Statistics__England_and_Wales_2018__1_.pdf

[153] Historical abortion statistics, United Kingdom (johnstonsarchive.net)

of life. Increasing promotion of abortion runs parallel to increasing promotion of euthanasia. In countries where euthanasia has been legalised, there is pressure for those laws to expand so that it should be available for non-terminal cases and for people who are suffering psychologically rather than physically, and even for those who are just "tired of life" after reaching 70 years of age.[154] There is now even world-wide public controversy and ethical debate over justifications for child euthanasia for those with grave illnesses or significant birth defects. Between 2016 and 2018, three children were euthanized in Belgium.[155] In the UK, the Royal College of Obstetricians and Gynaecologists has recommended that there be public debate around the option of non-resuscitation, withdrawal of treatment and even active euthanasia for the sickest of newborns. Arguments for child euthanasia include that it could save some families from years of emotional and financial suffering and could reduce the number of late abortions since parents would be, "more confident about continuing a pregnancy and taking a risk on the outcome." It has also been stated by Dr Pieter Sauer, co-author of the Dutch national guidelines on euthanasia of newborns, that British neonatologists already perform "mercy killings" and should be allowed to do so openly.[156]

It may be a statement of the obvious, but it is worth saying that while those who have already been born cannot be aborted, we are *all* potential recipients of euthanasia and assisted dying. So once we put

---

[154] https://adfinternational.org/commentary/euthanasia-a-new-lifestyle-choice/
[155] Child Euthanasia in Belgium | O'Neill Institute (georgetown.edu)
[156] https://en.wikipedia.org/wiki/Child_euthanasia

the innocent unborn in danger, the consequence is that we ourselves are at risk.

We have seen this idea played out in practice during the recent events and policies surrounding the Covid-19 pandemic, where some troubling assumptions about the value of the elderly and disabled have been displayed by elements within the NHS.

Normally, "Do Not Attempt Cardiopulmonary Resuscitation" (DNACPR) orders are enforced with the previous consent of patients or their family. During the early stages of the pandemic, however, blanket DNACPR orders were applied to groups of people, such as those with learning disabilities and the elderly, without their consent or that of their families. In a practice which is illegal, these orders were also placed on entire care homes.[157]

In addition to DNACPR orders being drawn up without consent, there is evidence of practitioners coercing and manipulating elderly, disabled and vulnerable people into agreeing to these orders. A Welsh GP surgery sent letters to high risk patients which advised them to complete a DNAR form to be applied if they contracted corona virus. It read "you are unlikely to receive hospital admission… and you certainly will not be offered a ventilator bed".[158]

There is no doubt that due to the extent of this policy, there must have been avoidable deaths of older or disabled people and those living in care homes. These concerns are so serious and widespread

---

[157] Covid-19: Care staff 'silenced' over inappropriate DNACPR orders | Nursing Times
[158] Whose life to save? Investigating the 'do not resuscitate' form coronavirus controversy - The Bristol Cable

that the government has asked the Care Quality Commission (CQC) to carry out a review of how DNACPR decisions were made, particularly during the early stages of the pandemic.

One of the main reasons behind the pushing of the abortion agenda is because of financial concerns. The same thinking is behind discrimination against elderly, disabled and vulnerable people during the Covid-19 pandemic. This should give us concern for our own ultimate welfare, regardless of our state of health. The devaluing of unborn human beings has opened the door to devaluing of every group of human beings which do not match up to perfection.

In the decades following the liberalisation of abortion laws in the UK we have witnessed the devaluing of marriage, a steep rise in divorce and the institution of gay marriage, which whether we like it or not, is contrary to Bible teaching. Our young people and children are targeted for false teaching on sexuality and morality.[159] There has been a collapse in our birth rate leading to an imbalance of generations, an overburdened working population requiring immigration to help support a larger proportion of elderly and consequent pressure for euthanasia of the elderly.

Finally, let's return for a moment to the concept of Gehenna, which we have seen was another name for the Valley of Slaughter. It

---

[159] At the end of its draft Guidance into Relationships and Sex and Relationships Education, the Government details '... the many excellent resources already available, free of charge, which schools can use to deliver the new curriculum. Under Sex Education, it includes examples such as www.sexwise.fpa.org.uk, and www.stonewall.org.uk/resources/different-families-same-love-pack and others. Nearly all promote sexual promiscuity, inclusivity, diversity, gender choice and so-called tolerance.

was historically where rubbish was thrown to be burnt, and it is hell, where the wicked were to be burnt.

On 21 October 1966, a mountain of rubbish from coal mining collapsed into a valley killing 116 children and 28 adults. This valley of slaughter was called Aberfan in Wales. It was the first televised national disaster in Britain. It was a devastating and shocking catastrophe which first destroyed the victims, then their families, then took the hope out of a village and finally put the whole nation into deep mourning. The scar was left on the families involved for the following generations.

The British "pro-choice" lobby refer to the abortion law, which was given royal assent on 27th October 1967 as being a great day of liberation for women and a landmark "human rights" victory. But presaging this event symbolically one year and one week before this was Aberfan. If we are in any doubt of God's opinion about this law, we have it demonstrated graphically and publicly here in such a calamitous event in British history.

Abortion is a hidden and secret disaster, the result of the supposed free choice of women, but it is no less devastating to those involved and to the nation than the public one seen on our television screens in the 1960s. Since 1967, it is estimated that there have been around 9 million abortions in the UK. We have not seen this on our television screens, but the Bible teaches us that each innocent cries out to God for justice. We must begin to view this issue with the eyes of the "God who sees," (**Ref Genesis 16.13)** rather than the superficial eyes of Man. This is part of the function and remit of the church.

**Without the right to life,
all other rights are meaningless**

10b: Deeper Reasons for Acceptance of Abortion

"We've distorted things to the point where people believe that anyone who opposes mothers killing their babies is waging war on women. How can we be so foolish to believe such a thing? One must be able to recognize the depravity to which we have sunken as a society when valuing baby's life is frowned upon."
Ben Carson (US politician)

We have seen that idolatry, which led to child sacrifice, became a progressively more common practice during the time of the kings of Israel and Judah. Child sacrifice was something that was totally opposed to the Law of God given to them through Moses. Idolatrous practices came in through connection and intermarriage with idolatrous nations, chief among them the Ammonites, whose god was Molech, a god who demanded propitiation through child sacrifice.

King David's son, Solomon, is often cited as having started the steady decline of the Israelites into idolatry. He had as many as 1000 wives and concubines, including the Ammonitess mother of his heir, Rehoboam. The Bible tells us that Solomon's many wives led him astray into idolatry, so that in the end he built high places for the worship of foreign gods including Molech:

Now King Solomon loved many foreign women:
…Moabite, Ammonite, Edomite, Sidonian,
and Hittite women,
from the nations concerning which
the LORD had said to the sons of Israel,

"You shall not associate with them,

nor shall they associate with you,

for they will surely turn your heart away

after their gods."

Solomon held fast to these in love.

He had seven hundred wives, princesses,

and three hundred concubines,

and his wives turned his heart away.

...For Solomon went after ...

Milcom the detestable idol of the Ammonites.

Solomon did what was evil in the sight of the LORD,

and did not follow the LORD *fully,*

...Then Solomon built a high place ...

for Molech the detestable idol of the sons of Ammon.

(1 Kings 11.1-7)

This was a very obvious flaw in Solomon's reign, but is this really the moment that worship of Molech began to be an influence on the people of Israel?

Solomon's father David was a "man after God's own heart".[160] Yet neither was King David faultless. He committed sexual sin with a married woman, then to cover it up he had the woman's husband murdered before it should be discovered that the woman was pregnant with his child. The Bible tells us that God's judgement on this situation was that the innocent child died.[161]

---

[160] **1 Samuel 13.14** and **Acts 13.22.**

Interestingly, immediately after this, King David went to complete the battle against the Ammonites which had been raging during all this time while he had been distracted by adultery and its consequences. He captured the Ammonite capital city, and crucially, removed the crown from the king's head and placed it on his own. Some translations say that he removed the crown from the head of the idol Milcom (Molech) and placed it on his own head.

This is the moment when the worship of Molech entered Jewish culture, when the crown passed from the head of the idol to the head of the king of Israel. And this happened immediately after the king had fallen into sexual sin which led to the conception and then death of a child, and the murder of the innocent husband. David was forgiven because he repented truly, but there were nevertheless consequences far beyond his own imagining, not just to himself or even to his own family, but to the nation which he led. These consequences can be represented by the new crown of authority which began to influence the kingdom from that moment onwards. This bejewelled gold headdress weighed 34 kilos.[162] It was a heavy burden to bear, as were the consequences of his sin. Because of his position as king, what he did in his private life and in secrecy had very obvious and public repercussions. The crown, apart from being a symbol of authority, is also a symbol of the new influence over the way the kings and their subjects thought: child sacrifice became something which was very difficult to rid the country of, not because

---

[161] **2 Samuel 11** and **1 Chronicles 20**
[162] **2 Samuel 12.30**

it served a useful or important role, but because the people's thinking had become clouded.

The result of all rejection of God is spiritual blindness.[163] In addition to this, we saw in **chapter 9a** that one of the effects on those who shed innocent blood is the loss of moral compass and a loss of peace.[164]

But Christ has made a way for this crown on our thinking to be removed and replaced by His Crown and His thinking. We have the capacity to have our mind renewed and transformed so that we can have a clear understanding of what is right and wrong, what is God's will and what is not.[165]

History and the Bible teach us that child sacrifice is part of the practice of witchcraft and idolatry (see **chapter 7**). It is the cause and consequence of the release of demonic powers in the nation.

In Britain, the **Witchcraft Act** was replaced in 1951 by the **Fraudulent Mediums Act**, an Act which protects against "fake witchcraft," while ignoring the danger of the genuine kind (presumably because it was assumed that this did not exist). This Fraudulent Mediums Act has now been absorbed into 2008 **EU consumer protection law**, which tells us that occult practices are now viewed as just another consumer transaction.

The Fraudulent Mediums Act was followed up by the **Obscene Publications Act in 1959, which** opened the door for legalisation of

[163] **2 Corinthians 4.4**
[164] **Isaiah 59.7-8**
[165] **Romans 12.2:** And do not be conformed to this world, but be transformed by the renewing of your mind, so that you may prove what is that good and acceptable and perfect will of God.

obscenity in publications, film and internet which we now consider the norm. The 2008 consumer protection law which included laws relating to occult practices, was followed six years later in the UK by the introduction of gay marriage.

Although we in the West are used to considering idolatry as something to do with pagan religious ceremonies, we must come to terms with the fact that putting anything above God in importance in our lives is idolatry and even if it appears to us to be benign, it must ultimately be destructive.

We have seen that modern idols (reasons for abortion) can include fear, lifestyle, sexual sin, financial and career freedom, along with scientific advancement, (see **chapter 7**) and many more reasons which I have not included here. These modern idols are ultimately the idol of self or "me". Scripture makes the connection between materialism and idolatry.[166]

Materialism, along with consumerism and all that accompany them are no neutral phenomenon, or inescapable fact of life, but they are the modern face of greed, envy and selfishness which have become so normalised in our society that we may not even perceive them anymore. But we perceive their consequences. They represent a principality against which the church must stand.

As we saw in **chapter 2**, one of the key reasons for the increasing acceptance and normalisation of abortion is the undervaluing of human beings per se, so that humanity is often considered to be of no

---

[166] **Ephesians 5.5:** For this you know with certainty, that no sexually immoral or impure or greedy person, which amounts to an idolater, has an inheritance in the kingdom of Christ and God.

more value than animal life, or even that human beings are a plague on the earth. One of the key underlying reasons for this is decades of promotion in schools and universities of evolution to explain the source of life. Yet the Bible tells us that this too is idolatry.[167]

We are told that by being idolaters, people turn away from God and from all mercy and love.[168]

Since God IS love, turning away from Him means we turn away from love, and then we begin stumbling and forgetting fundamental truths, wandering into error.[169]

What a person believes, the god you follow, affects *you*, your identity and how you view others. Idolatry makes a person begin to consider themselves and then others as being worthless.[170]

2 kings 17.15 may express this point better in the Amplified Version:

They rejected His statutes and His covenant
which He made with their fathers,
as well as His warnings that he gave them.

---

[167] **Romans 1.25**...because [by choice] they exchanged the truth of God for a lie, and worshiped and served the creature rather than the Creator...[AMP]

[168] **Jonah 2.8:** Those who regard and follow worthless idols turn away from their [living source of] mercy and lovingkindness. [AMP]

[169] **Jeremiah 18.15:** For My people have forgotten Me, they burn incense to worthless gods and they have stumbled from their ways, from the ancient paths, to walk in bypaths, not on a highway.

[170] **2 kings 17.15:** What fault did your ancestors find in me, that they strayed so far from me? They followed worthless idols and became worthless themselves. **Jeremiah 2.6:** They rejected his decrees and the covenanthe had made with their ancestors and the statutes he had warned them to keep. They followed worthless idols and themselves became worthless. [NIV]

And they followed vanity [that is, false gods, idols]
and became vain (empty-headed).
They followed the [pagan practices of the] nations
which surrounded them,
although the LORD had commanded
that they were not to do as they did. (AMP)

So rejection of ourselves and of others is what makes abortion, (the unthinkable), become thinkable.

We are told that comparing abortion to the holocaust is a provocative and emotive argument. But we need look no further than the use by scientists and other industries of the tissue of the aborted unborn. This is compelling evidence pointing to the obvious and unavoidable conclusion that the holocaust analogy fits perfectly.

We are quick to condemn wartime atrocities perpetrated by other societies and to think that because of the passage of time and our new technologies, we are somehow more "advanced" then they. But our technological advancement has simply become a blindfold so that we cannot see the idolatrous state we are really in. It causes us to accept the logic of modern promotion of abortion which we have come to accept as a solution to the problems in which we find ourselves. This shows us the true nature of our society.

Chapter 11: A Church Issue

11a: A Church Failure

"I want to say that in the period that lies ahead, the only safety for every believer will be to deliberately and purposely align yourself with God's purposes and priorities."
Derek Prince

The Evangelical Alliance commissioned a questionnaire which was filled out by Christians in Britain. In answer to the statement "abortion can never be justified" respondents were completely split across the spectrum in their level of agreement. Around 20% entirely agreed with the statement, around 20% entirely disagreed with the statement, and opinions were fairly evenly distributed across the spectrum of approval and disapproval.[171] Notice that these percentages are similar to responses made by people outside the church. It seems logical to conclude that since the church is in fact thinking in the same way as the world, it is probably also acting in the same way too. So we have an urgent need for repentance within the church.

"You shall love the Lord your God with all your heart, and with all your soul, and with all your strength, and with all your mind; and your neighbour as yourself".[172] We know that loving God includes and is demonstrated by how we love our neighbour. This is because

---

[171] www.eauk.org/church/resources/snapshot/upload/21st-Century-Evangelicals.pdf
[172] **Luke 10.27**

our neighbour is made in the image of God. The unborn have been described by supporters of abortion as being less than human, or of less value than others, but we have seen that they are entirely human and of just as much value as anyone else. Thus they are our neighbour. So, with this in mind, how should we respond to abortion? Jesus explained this using the parable of the Good Samaritan (**Luke 10.30-37**).

A person was attacked and his life put in jeopardy because of the actions of violent thieves. Two passers-by, who were religious people, and considered that they loved God, did not stop to assist. They may have felt sorry for the victim, and expressed pity. They may have been "anti-robbery" and lamented the fact that this had happened, saying that they would never choose robbery themselves. But they were busy with the requirements of their religion. To make themselves ceremonially unclean by touching a potentially dead body would mean that they would have to give up seven days from their calendar of activities in order to help this person and then become ceremonially clean again.

But Jesus said that these religious people, who were intent on following the rules of their religion, missed the very point which underpinned it. He said that the one who was a neighbour to the injured man was the one who *acted* with mercy, the one who sacrificed something in order to help him. The Samaritan sacrificed his time, his comfort and his money in order to save his neighbour from death. This is how he demonstrated his love for God, in taking care of the needs of someone who was not considered by others to be worth helping.

Individual churches have missions, activities, programmes, priorities, and specific focuses. We find ourselves busy with many activities which God has called us to do, and which are good in themselves. Yet, when we walk past the injured victim of robbery in the street, our first priority must be to assist that person. Our first priority must be care for the one whose life is in danger, who has been attacked by law-breakers. Otherwise we would become like the Pharisees and hypocrites, criticised by Jesus for worrying about the details of our religion while neglecting "...the weightier provisions of the law: justice and mercy and faithfulness." Jesus said that we need to do the other things too, but "these are the things you should have done without neglecting the others".[173] We are commanded to love our neighbour as ourselves.[174] This command has no limitation, distinctions, or exclusions and it includes our unborn neighbours. Loving them "as yourself" doesn't just mean to the same degree, it means you first recognise them as being as much a person as yourself.

Although Lot was a "righteous man"[175] he chose to live close to the unrighteous.[176] He was attracted to material prosperity, ease and comfort, but ignored the corrupting effect it would have on himself and his family (leading to the loss of his wife and two sons-in-law).

---

[173] **Matthew 23.23**.
[174] **Leviticus 19.18:** ... you shall love your neighbor as yourself; I am the LORD.
[175] **2 Peter 2.8**
[176] **Genesis 13.12-13**

Christians and churches that focus on their own well-being and material prosperity will lose out in the same way as our prototype Lot.

Later on in the Bible, Solomon married women of neighbouring countries who followed other religions and thus ended up mixing the worship of God with the worship of idols including Molech. He led the country to do the same. So by comparison, if the church dilutes or compromises the Word of God, then we know that heathen practices will enter one way or another. We may say that we represent Jesus to the world but in fact that representation must be tarnished.

The Bible refers many times to our life with God as beginning with being "born again".[177] Just as God ordains that a person be born again spiritually, He ordains that a person be born first physically. Satan wants to destroy that new birth, but if our life is put into God's hands He will bring it to full term, to ripeness and fruition. This can only happen if He is allowed in. Our prayer needs to be "Your will be done on earth as it is in heaven," in the physical as it is in the spiritual.

From a realization of the nature of God, and then the intrinsic worth of human beings (and of ourselves in particular) flows everything else. The fact that militant abortionist ideology is so vocal and successful in the West today comes from the basic self-loathing encouraged by our society. It has gained traction because ours is a culture which teaches that all human beings are not created equal. The legality of abortion up to the time of birth of even the mildly disabled is testimony to this. We are taught that we are not created at all but are descended from animals and are therefore worth the same or less

---

[177] **John 3.3, 3.7, 1 Peter 1.3, 1.23**

than them. The propagation of evolutionism to explain our identity means that the very basis for all morality is undercut. If we are purely biological beings no different in nature from all other animals, then we should expect nothing more from ourselves and other humans than we expect from those animals. There is no such thing as freedom of choice since all is founded on biology and neuroscience.[178] This means that in effect, there is no right and wrong, and the only basis for action should be self-preservation.

The church in general has failed to effectively teach Biblical values regarding sexual purity even to our congregations, often unconsciously taking our cues from the culture around us rather than from God, not even considering that the apparently advanced nature of that culture hides the fact that it has lapsed into a form of paganism. We have not taught effectively about the love of God, which is a jealous love of *all* His children which is stronger than death, as demonstrated by his crucifixion and resurrection. If this were fully understood by believers, then we would not be afraid to condemn abortion from the pulpit and it would not be taboo in our congregations. There is only a fierce justification for abortion available in the world because without Christ, once we admit the seriousness of our faults there can be no forgiveness. Once we admit that abortion is murder then all the world has to offer is condemnation. The Christian church needs to be unafraid to offer the forgiveness available at the Cross, which requires the recognition of sin.

---

[178] There's No Such Thing as Free Will | Richard Dawkins Foundation

One of the functions of the church is to do what is described in **Proverbs 31.8-9**:

Open your mouth for the people who cannot speak,
For the rights of all the unfortunate.
Open your mouth, judge righteously,
And defend the rights of the poor and needy.

The (Protestant) church in Britain, far from speaking up coherently with one voice for the voiceless, has remained largely silent on the issue of abortion. When we consider the colossal importance of this subject along with its widespread practice and acceptance, this is an extremely serious matter which has already had devastating consequences. David Brennan, of Brephos and CBR has said, "The church is sleep-walking through the greatest human rights injustice the world has ever seen."[179] The church's silence on this subject is not a neutral silence. It communicates to those within the church who have had an abortion that they have committed an unforgiveable sin. That silence also communicates to the world that we either have no opinion or that we approve abortion. It communicates that we have nothing to offer those who are suffering the consequences of abortion, or feeling that they have no option but to have one. The hand that should be extended to the world in assistance and forgiveness is kept in our pocket.

---

[179] See: www.brephos.org

We must be the head rather than the tail being wagged by materialism, secular humanism, evolutionism, feminism, environmentalism, individualism and every other fashionable "'ism". If we are afraid to offend we must beware draining the Gospel of its power to heal and redeem *all* sin. Scripture warns us that we can become a church having a form of godliness but denying its power.[180] If we find that our prayers for revival seem to be landing on deaf ears, then we must ask ourselves if passivity and even acceptance of the sin of abortion, as well as a lack of assistance for those struggling in this area, may be a hindrance to our prayers.

It is estimated that there are 125,000 abortions worldwide per day, nearly 87 per minute (the true figure being certainly many more than this). Since we know that each murdered innocent has a voice before God, this means there is a constant clamorous cacophony of innocent children's voices calling out for justice to the God who hears, who never sleeps and who is a God of justice precisely *because* He is a God of Love.

When we consider it in this light, the issue of abortion becomes far more than the optional side issue which the church has considered it, but rather something which needs to be of supreme concern to the church, as it is to God.

---

[180] **cf. 2 Timothy 3.5**

11b: A Church Opportunity

Let's get to the solution and to the good news.

In the time of Jonah, Nineveh was a wicked place, ruled by violence which included, as in today's Britain, injustice, murder and the subjugation of the weakest. Jonah disobeyed God out of fear and did not go to the city to give them the warning of imminent wrath of God, but rather he went in the opposite direction.

The first step to correcting this, as always, was repentance. Interestingly, the circumstances of Jonah's repentance (being in the belly of a fish) were comparable to being in the womb, or in the grave.[181] It was an entirely hopeless and entirely vulnerable situation to be in.

To Jonah's surprise, God had prepared the hearts of the Ninevites to receive the word of warning, and they repented on mass.[182] So God saw their repentance and did not destroy them.

Not only does God forgive the worst sin and the worst sinner, but He goes out of His way to search out the sinner to save us, giving each of us an opportunity to repent. He gives His church the possibility to repent and begin to speak out against even culturally acceptable sins. We should not be surprised or hurt if the response to our warnings is aggressive persecution, accusations of bigotry, emotionalism, "hating women" etc. On the other hand, we may be

---

[181] **Jonah 2.2**: I called out of my distress to the LORD, and He answered me. I cried for help from the depth of Sheol; You heard my voice.
[182] **Jonah 3.5**: Then the people of Nineveh believed in God; and they called a fast and put on sackcloth from the greatest to the least of them.

surprised, as Jonah was, to find that He has prepared the hearts of the people for repentance. Our only responsibility is to give the message as Jonah did, since the rest is the responsibility of God.

Since abortion is the sacrifice of an innocent, the Gospel alternative to it is another sacrifice: "Take, eat; this is My body... Drink from it, all of you; for this is My blood of the covenant, which is poured out for many for forgiveness of sins".[183] Our Saviour chose to give his life, no one made him do it and no one took his life from him. It was his voluntary self-sacrifice.

A predisposition towards self-sacrifice is a requirement for every parent, but is something that has become foreign to our culture, culminating in the promotion of abortion on demand without restriction as a woman's right. Yet it was a foundational part of the culture of many nations, including Britain, not so long ago. A good illustration of this is a story recorded by the Society for the Protection of Unborn Children (SPUC):

Five members of Mary Connor's family fought in the First World War, only one of them returning home. The others all died on the battlefield. Mary treasured their medals and war records for years as a testimony to the sacrifice they made for the freedom and wellbeing of the generations yet to come. Then, a century after her relatives went off to war and gave their lives for the sake of those who had not yet been born, Mary and her husband decided to sell the medals to donate the proceeds to SPUC. The reason for her gift was that she felt that

---

[183] **Mathew 26.26-27**

her relatives would have approved since they shared the same values of self-sacrifice and protection of the innocent.[184]

Here we can tell the bond that connects the pro-life movement with the generations who came before us. The sacrifice of these brave men has been betrayed in a terrible way by those who push abortion for financial or ideological motives, who in the process scorn the sacrifices of the past. But the selfless attitude of the First World War foot soldier is a shadow or echo which points us to the reality of the self-sacrifice which Christ demonstrated and modeled to us, and which is expressed in the actions of a truly Christ-centred church.

Repentance starts with the church. Once this is done the church can fulfil her role as she was meant to. Abortion culture is about sacrificing the lives of others. We are to be imitators of Christ, following in His example and laying down our own priorities, our comfort, our reputations, our church programmes, our success and our selves down to serve the Lord. This is one way in which we worship God, and this is a great part of the function of the church.[185]

As a consequence of knowing who we are, as image-bearers of God and representatives of Christ, we will not only care for the poor, fight human trafficking, claim the dignity of the elderly and disabled and advocate for immigrants, we will not only lobby and fight for

---

[184] https://www.spuc.org.uk/News/ID/384182/The-WWI-medals-funding-SPUCs-work

[185] **Ephesians 5.1-2:** Therefore be imitators of God, as beloved children; and walk in love, just as Christ also loved you and gave Himself up for us, an offering and a sacrifice to God as a fragrant aroma. **Romans 12.1:** Therefore I urge you, brothers and sisters, by the mercies of God, to present your bodies as a living and holy sacrifice, acceptable to God, which is your spiritual service of worship.

religious liberty. We will fight against the very first and most grievous attack on our fellow human beings, that of abortion. We will do all this out of love for God and concern for those who bear His sacred image.[186]

These words were spoken by Jesus to His generation to say that there was no excuse for those who lived beside Him since the Ninevites who were given much less revelation were still able to repent. According to the same principle, our generation today, which knows so much and which chooses to close its eyes to so much, will also be judged far more severely than those who acted in ignorance.

The Lord constrains Himself to work through His church, so if we do nothing, nothing will be done. If we do not repent, He cannot forgive and set us free, if we do not pray, angels cannot be dispatched, if we say nothing then the Accuser's voice shouting his condemnation and fear will be the only voice which vulnerable women hear. If we do not give practical help to those who feel their only option is abortion, or to those suffering its consequences, then that practical help will not be given.

The church has a responsibility before God to rescue those in danger, to:

Rescue those who are being taken away to death,
And those who are staggering to the slaughter,

---

[186] **Matthew 12.41:** "The men of Nineveh will stand up as witnesses at the judgment against this generation, and will condemn it because they repented at the preaching of Jonah; and now, something greater than Jonah is here." [AMP]

*Oh hold them back! (**Proverbs 24.11**)*

The church must be a beacon, pointing the way to God, and pointing the way to assistance and Salvation.

We can help or point the way to post and pre-abortion counselling, or with practical needs including housing, benefits, clothing, education and employment. We can help by adopting or fostering, demonstrating to the world that we value all human beings regardless of inauspicious beginnings. If this is not possible, we can support those who do this. We can lobby government and speak out publically so that the noisy "pro-choice" shouting is not the only voice heard.

We have a choice to make: we can passively accept that this issue is far too huge, far too delicate an issue to touch. We can decide to give up because there are far too few people fighting for the life of the unborn, compared to a multi-million pound celebrity and media-endorsed Goliath abortion industry. We can decide that too few people are standing against this giant so we can do nothing. If so, we must consider God's warning to those who ignore the needy, as expressed in **Proverbs 24.12**:

If you say, "See, we did not know this,"
Does He who weighs the hearts not consider it?
And does He who watches over your soul not know it?
And will He not repay a person according to his work?

Alternatively we can decide that when there is no hope according to our human understanding, this is precisely when we need to give this to God and ask Him what each of us is called to do in response to this need.

Will we as the church come into agreement with the heart of God? It has been said many times that our generation's Auschwitz is in the womb of women. We are silent participants if we stand by and do nothing.

Lord, show us
what must be done

Appendices: Useful information

1: Interview with Dave Brennan, of Brephos

Brephos (www.brephos.org) is a ministry dedicated to equipping and motivating churches to speak out for the unborn, with the aim of every church speaking out against abortion so that it becomes unthinkable. It is a project of CBRUK (the Centre for Bio-ethical Reform) which is an organisation whose aim is to make abortion unthinkable to society by exposing it for what it is.

In your discussions with pastors and church ministers, what kinds of feelings have you found that they have about pro-life issues?

Among pastors and ministers I have found a real mix of views. One reason for this may be that the issue is not being taught much in seminaries.

Some pastors of the more conservative churches are notionally pro-life but not many are teaching their congregations on the subject. A pastor often assumes, without asking his congregants, that they must be all be pro-life simply because he is pro-life, but we know that this is often not the case.

Those ministers and pastors on the more liberal wing of the church are more difficult to engage with. Pastors of these churches are generally not pro-life. But even in the evangelical scene, some pastors are on the pro-choice side of the argument, claiming that it's a grey issue.

It's clear that fear stops many from speaking out – they fear causing damage or upset, and they fear putting people off their church or the gospel.

Some pastors feel convicted to speak out but are just overwhelmed – they don't know where to begin and they feel under-equipped. That's one of the reasons we exist – to help churches to do this.

I recently visited Bristol Christian Union, where one of the Christian leaders told me that there would be a range of views on abortion within the CU – and for that reason they wouldn't speak about it. This is fairly typical of the state of affairs in the Christian Unions of our universities, and also many churches.

I find that churches teach on, and are generally clear on the importance of evangelism and Christian charity, but they are not clear about what they should think about abortion. Well known Christian leaders won't talk about abortion because it's controversial. Unfortunately, the end result is that there is a kind of fog where people don't know what to think because there is an absence of leadership on this issue.

What would you say is the cause of the church in Britain's failure to engage on this issue?

I think that this is because the modern church has lost the art of engaging in controversy, of confronting sin in all its forms and calling out the nation which has fallen deep into sin, calling the nation to repentance.

In part this because we don't even call ourselves, one another, to repentance. If we don't repent, how can we call the nation to repentance!

The methodology of our evangelism is that it must be seeker-sensitive and avoid offense. These man-made rules of methodology, which contrast with what was practiced in biblical and early church times, have become an untouchable law, a pharisaic tradition whose goal is to protect the church's reputation at all costs so that the church looks attractive and easy. Pro-life teaching against abortion jars with the seeker-friendly approach.

I am concerned that what masquerades as pastoral sensitivity or an evangelistic methodology is in fact fear of man and persecution-avoidance – we don't want trouble, so we keep quiet about abortion.

How do you see the general state of the church in the UK in relation to God?

Big question! Right now, for the most part, I see the state of the Church in the UK as being a mirror of the state in which Israel found herself at moments in the Old Testament. The people of God copied the practices of the nations around them, practices which culminated in child sacrifice. This is expressed in Psalm 106, for example. God's response towards his people was one of disgust. We see, for example in the book of Jeremiah, how God puts up with the sin of His people until a final straw causes His anger to overflow – that final straw seems to be idolatry mixed with child sacrifice. Ezekiel 20 shows how, at that point, God wouldn't listen anymore to the prayers of His people, because they remained stubbornly unrepentant of child sacrifice. Verse 31 makes this clear: "'For when you offer your gifts and make your sons pass through fire, you defile yourselves with all your idols, even to this day. So shall I be enquired of by you, O house of Israel? As I live' says the Lord God, 'I will not be inquired of by you.'"

Everyone wants to see revival but I fear that very few really dare to ask what's blocking it. I don't think there's one answer to that, but when you consider God's reaction to child sacrifice in the Old Testament – and when you consider that abortion is modern-day child sacrifice, and it's in the Church, and we're tolerating it – how could God grant revival to us unless we repent of abortion?

Tragically, some in the Church appear to think that the key to revival is the very opposite – to become even more like the world around us, even more culturally assimilated.

How have you found the response in the churches where you have been given the opportunity to give a presentation?

The difficulty with talking to the church about the subject of abortion is getting a platform to speak in the first place. Once pastors make space, I have found the response to be overwhelmingly positive: there is conviction and some respond, but the problem is getting the platform to be able to speak in the first place.

Almost every Sunday that I've spoken in a church, someone has come up to me who's had an abortion, and they thank me and often say it's the first time they've ever heard it spoken about in church. There must be tens of thousands of Christians in the country who've had abortions and are waiting for someone to speak into it – and tens of thousands more who are likely to go on and have abortions unless we do something.

The gospel is big enough for this issue, and the Holy Spirit is powerful enough. We have to believe that. We have good news and we can help by speaking the truth in love.

So what should pastors and leaders in the church do?

The pastor's role is to equip the saints for service. They need to shepherd those they are responsible for, safeguarding them against satanic ideologies, including the ideology of abortion. The pastor's role is to lead from the front rather than to be afraid to touch this key part of modern life.

So specifically, pastors need to teach regularly on the subject and encourage the congregation to respond in action. Bringing this subject out of the closet and talking about it from the pulpit is what gives church members permission and blessing to move forward on this subject.

At the time of the interview, church leaders are providing very proactive leadership and teaching on how to respond to the Covid-19 pandemic, giving the lead on how we must not be afraid but trust God alone for our health, our protection and our future. But we need basic leadership on the subject of abortion, and we need to be more action-focused regarding this.

Many pastors can feel ill-equipped to talk about abortion but in fact their role isn't to have all the answers or to have specialised knowledge, but rather it's just to teach the word of God, rely on the Holy Spirit, and point people in the right direction – to specialised help where appropriate – and we can help with that.

One place that they can direct people is towards CBRUK (the Centre for Bioethical Reform). Brephos is part of CBRUK, which is an organisation whose overall aim is to end abortion. The organisation trains up activists, educates the public, goes into schools to educate students; all this to challenge assumptions and the way people think. We also have Post-Abortion Support for Everyone, which has an amazing gospel-centred Recovery Course for use in churches, and we are in the process of launching HOPE Pregnancy Centre.

This leads us to the question of why the pro-life lobby has been so ineffectual so far in combating abortion. Why do you think this is?

CBR has studied the history of social reform such as the process by which the Transatlantic Slave Trade was banned in the nineteenth century. The conclusion of those studies was that success only comes from exposing injustice to the light of day. So when the new nineteenth century technology of photography was used to demonstrate the way children were being exploited in factories, and the inhumane way black slaves were being treated, both practices came quickly to an end. Images of the real lives of real human beings made people understand that these issues affected real human beings. Both practices had been allowed to carry on for years because of the ability of proponents to dehumanise those affected, but the photographs humanised the victims and made both practices unthinkable and unacceptable to society. Similarly with abortion, there is no way to get rid of it other than by showing the reality of what it is.

Sadly much of the pro-life movement has made the same mistake over and over: we have recoiled from the difficult, unpopular, but utterly essential work of exposing the horror of abortion, and instead we have expressed our opinions. No one cares about our opinions; without exposing abortion for what it is, showing it to be *objectively* horrific and inhumane, we will simply be considered old-fashioned and irrelevant for our out-of-sync opinions.

This is why CBRUK's methodology is to use imagery to show what abortion actually is, to show the victim thereby humanising him or her in the same way that abolitionists did with black slaves. Imagery cuts through all the arguments and justifications for abortion, because it shows that we are dealing with a human being who deserves respect and care, not a lump of cells or a "pre-human".

One of the aims of CBR is to train up activists so that they can go into the street and into schools. It gives training in apologetics, with the whole aim of doing a mass public education campaign. CBR also does post-abortion support and at the time of the interview are about to open the new project "HOPE" which is a gospel-centred, evangelistic, life-affirming model of pregnancy centre whose focus is specifically on outreach, taking the gospel to those who have had an abortion, or those who are considering it.

Where people tend to go wrong once they want to get active on this subject is that they think about what skill set they have and what they like and don't like doing. What we need to be doing is exposing the reality of abortion.

Pastors can invite a CBR speaker to give a talk at their church about what social reformers have done throughout history, and to raise the profile of this kind of activity in the church.

What would you say to Christians who would say that abortion and pro-life issues are a sideline to the main function of the church?

I would say that if we sideline this issue in church, then we and the church itself will become sidelined in society. By absenting ourselves from the discourse, we make the church become impotent and irrelevant. There is a desperate need for the church to get off the fence and engage in this issue, but at the moment this is not happening to any great extent. We must remember that if we take the risk of proclaiming the truth, God is faithful to those who take that step of faith.

Martin Luther said "If I profess with loudest voice and clearest exposition every portion of the truth of God except that little point which the world and the devil are at the moment attacking, I am not confessing Christ, however boldly I may be professing Christ. Where the battle rages, there the loyalty of the soldier is proved, and to be steady on all the battlefield besides, is mere flight and disgrace if he flinches at that point."

We could also consider Bonhoeffer's witness against the persecution of Jews within and without the Church: he saw this as an essential, gospel issue in his context. We look back and admire him now, but are we following in his footsteps with today's pressing issue?

Abortion is the greatest ethical issue of our day. We can proclaim that Jesus opposes racism and not expect persecution because this battle has already been fought and won by the generations who preceded us, so that racism is generally rejected by society. But to proclaim that Jesus opposes abortion is not generally accepted because this battle has yet to be won. When we proclaim this we can expect to be the target of persecution, and it is precisely by that persecution that we know we are His.

The Church in the West has generally become averse to persecution, and to think that those who come under fire must be in the wrong. We think that if the world doesn't like our message then we must have got the message wrong. But God says that we are blessed when we are persecuted.

This is a defining issue for the church. It is also a revival issue. If we want revival then we must first have repentance. God requires repentance in the church because we have come to mirror the state in which Israel found herself in the Old Testament. How can we go out to the world and confront sin when that sin is also inside the church?

But the hope is that even though we may be compromised and lacking in saltiness, once we repent, God is gracious to restore us.

Let's look for a moment at the British church's general response to the national crisis caused by Covid-19, the Corona Virus. Not only have we seen creative responses to the ban on public gatherings (live streamed services and the like): countless bespoke messages have addressed the phenomenon of the coronavirus head on, offering a Christian response specifically to this crisis. And words are being matched with action. The very *fact* that churches are responding to corona so decisively is noteworthy. It shows that we *can* do it. One might surmise from the decades of inaction and silence on, for example, 9 million slaughtered babies, that the Church is quite unable or unwilling to respond to anything – but corona is showing us that this is not the case. Where there is the will or the compulsion, the Church can indeed jump to it.

The fact that we are responding so resolutely to corona, whilst continuing to ignore abortion, ought to drive us to ask some searching questions of ourselves.

2: Helpful Organisations

What to do if You are a Church Member, Minister or Leader

It is all very well diagnosing the problem but how should we deal with it? The more we learn about the situation in the UK and in fact in the world generally regarding abortion, the more we realise just how much work there is to be done. In the face of such a challenge it is easy to be overwhelmed and neutralised, wondering how anything an individual or even a single congregation, can do would make any difference to such multi-million-pound, media and politician-endorsed mammoth. The answer is that we can do nothing without the power of God, and nothing if we do not work together.

So now that we have discussed **why** the church needs to be at the forefront of protection of the unborn, let us look at the vital question of **how** we need to go about this effectively.

Repentance in the Church

Before repentance can be preached to the world, repentance is required within the church. To achieve this:

Prayer

This is required from those who have become aware of the importance of this subject; prayer for repentance in the church, but also prayer for those who preach and teach in the church to become aware of the seriousness of the situation and the Church's responsibility to tackle the issue.

There are many reasons that church leaders may have for not wanting to even mention the subject of the sanctity of life within the church. Some are because of errors in thinking, others are legitimate concerns. The fear of appearing unloving, or feeling ill-equipped to deal with the sensitivities and complexities of the subject, these are legitimate concerns. There is a potential to cause much damage if we approach the subject without wisdom or in a judgemental way. Churches have been known to split over far less contentious issues than abortion, so fears of causing divisions among the fellowship are legitimate. But these are a challenge to prayer and planning rather than a reason to avoid the subject.

There are some more serious problems in our churches which need to be dealt with in prayer before we can be effective. Some members in our churches, and even in leadership, may not be sure that abortion is wrong. Many professing Christians have the same attitude towards abortion as do the majority of unbelievers. This should not be so, but it is currently the case in parts of the professing church. This is a stronghold which needs to be broken.

The focus of our congregations may be so much on being "seeker-friendly" that we fear that the appearance of being judgemental might upset outreach and put people off. We may think that if someone had an abortion before they came to salvation, they are forgiven automatically as a part of their salvation, so there is no need to "rake up" the past. Finally, since abortion is such a taboo it is easy to conclude that it does not exist in a particular congregation, or that Christians just don't have abortions. These are all strongholds of wrong thinking, and I am sure there may be many more, which need to be torn down in concerted, tactical prayer before ever a word is preached.

We have seen throughout preceding chapters of this book that abortion has always been connected to occult activity. This is not a condemnation of the women involved but an observation regarding societies throughout history which accept and promote the murder of the innocent young, be it in biblical Israel or in modern Britain. Abortion represents a powerful spiritual stronghold which must be overcome first and foremost in the spiritual realm by prayer in an organised way by a united, repentant and focussed church.

Preaching of the Sanctity of Life

This must be from the pulpit, by leadership rather than members of the congregation, since the protection of the unborn is a central Gospel issue, and must be recognised as such rather than being relegated to the fringes. A whole Sunday morning needs to be diarised for teaching the congregation about abortion so that it is heard by everyone. This is a challenge and requires a sacrifice.

If it seems too delicate an issue to approach, one solution may be to invite a specialist teacher to your church.

One organization which can help with this is Brephos. (www.brephos.org)

This is a Christian organisation, focused on equipping and encouraging the church to mobilise in protection of the unborn. It provides speakers which churches can invite for a Sunday morning presentation to the church on the issue of abortion, thus breaking the silence on the issue within church. It also offers training on how to deal with the topic sensitively and Biblically both within the church and in evangelism.

A Post-Abortion Course Within the Church

This is another important step to take, so that the many believing Christians who still suffer post abortion symptoms and guilt can find true forgiveness and freedom in this particular area. In order to help others, we need to find full freedom ourselves. Brephos can give advice regarding setting this up. A partner organisation called PASE, (Post Abortion Support for Everyone,) can also assist. (See: www.postabortsupport.com)

Promoting Fostering and Adoption Within the Church

Churches can encourage this as an outworking of our Christian faith and a demonstration that we really do believe that every life is valuable and worth cherishing, regardless of inauspicious beginnings. One of the sometimes legitimate charges levelled against Christians regarding abortion is that we "tell women what to do but do nothing to help." Perhaps the modern church could take a leaf from the book of the early Christians who rescued infants – mainly girls, the sick and deformed – who had been left exposed to die by their pagan neighbours. The modern equivalent to this could be fostering and adoption. Most children in the care system are there for the same reasons that abortion occurs, so we need to show by our actions that these children are valued after all, whether girl or boy, disabled or from an ethnic minority, whatever their background. Adoption and fostering are not a thing for the faint-hearted, especially for Christians facing a politically-correct social care system, but there are Christian organisations which can help support people in the adoption and fostering process.

The Church as Signpost

If care for the unborn, as well as for vulnerable women and children, become prominently on the agenda in our churches, then we can become a sign post, a place where people in difficulty come to be pointed in the right direction to receive help. Many people choose abortion out of panic, and because they are unaware of the assistance which is already available to them. The abortion industry is powerful and wealthy, so it often appears that they are the only ones available to deal with a crisis pregnancy. But this is not the case. There is much work already being done, behind the scenes and without fanfare, to assist people in having their child rather than an abortion. The Church can be a place where people go to find out where specialist help can be obtained. We can be a signpost, as well as a place to go to find forgiveness and restoration. If the church in general became synonymous with help during crisis then the first place people go to deal with a crisis pregnancy would be the church rather than a panicked visit to an abortion clinic.

Signposts for Assistance Post Abortion:

Here are some of the organisations which can help if you are facing emotional difficulties after an abortion:

The Pregnancy Crisis Helpline

www.pregnancycrisishelpline.org.uk

This is a phone counselling organisation whose remit includes supporting women post abortion. They have a registry of local services.

Life Charity

https://lifecharity.org.uk/

This is for post abortion counselling. They also have a registry of local services for face-to-face support.

Arch

https://www.archtrust.org.uk

This is the sister organization to SPUC (The Society for the Protection of Unborn Children). ARCH offers help for women, men and families to restore their lives and relationships after an abortion experience.

Post Abort Support

www.postabortsupport.com

www.facebook.com/PostAbortionSupportforEveryone

This is a support group for anyone who's been hurt as a result of abortion (mothers, fathers, siblings, friends, clinic workers etc). It describes itself as a safe place to share what is often a secret anguish and encourage one another as we recover. It is a Christian organisation dedicated to increasing the understanding of how abortion affects those involved and encourage everyone to be brave enough to be open to helping their friends through to healing.

The philosophy is to facilitate good helpful healing relationships that will give post-abortive people the support and care to assist them in their recovery, to help those affected by abortion see clearly what they have done, and choose a healthy way to recover. They do not do counselling.

Her Choice to Heal

https://herchoicetoheal.com/

This is a Christian American website dedicated to abortion recovery. It contains an online abortion course which may be useful to some people who do not want to talk to a person about the subject. It contains information about post-abortion PTSD and psychological harms of abortion.

Signposts for someone with an Unplanned Pregnancy

The church can assist on a personal level, and we can also point the way to specialised assistance. One organisation which can assist when someone has an unplanned pregnancy is:

The Pregnancy Crisis Helpline: www.pregnancycrisishelpline.org.uk This organization offers support for women (and their partners) struggling with an unplanned pregnancy, but they do not refer people for abortion.

Since the first reaction to an unplanned pregnancy is often to panic, people can hurry into action which they later regret. The helpline seeks to support women and their partners in exploring their feelings and their options at this stressful time.

The Pregnancy Crisis Helpline also has access to an extensive directory of pregnancy support centres around the UK, and can tell you about your local services so you can receive face-to-face support in your local area. People can receive help locally through **counselling and financial advice**, they can have help with **housing**, and there are **support groups** for single parents and many others.

The Pregnancy crisis helpline is a one-stop helpline which connects people to local help where they are.

Help with Practical and Financial Matters

A useful organization is Life charity; (https://lifecharity.org.uk) which helps people in a crisis pregnancy right up until the child is 4. Assistance includes **counselling, housing**, **training** in parenting skills as well as **free pregnancy tests**, **baby equipment** and **emotional support**. Assistance includes **practical support, clothing** etc. The organisation supports **houses** in most areas of England for mothers supporting a child in difficult circumstances.

Training in Counselling

This is available from:

https://lifecharity.org.uk

www.pregnancycrisishelpline.org.uk

There is a need for more volunteers to be trained listeners. This is not about being a counselor, but is mostly about listening and connecting people with the help they need, and learning what **not** to say. So you can help by simply being on the end of the phone.

Intercession

Most of the organisations mentioned here are either overtly Christian or staffed mainly by believers, and would appreciate prayer support from the church. This is something anyone can do at any time.

For doctors:

You can contact the Society for the Protection of Unborn Children:

https://www.spuc.org.uk/

This is an organization which supports doctors who are standing up for life against the pressures they face.

For teachers:

Contact the Society for the Protection of Unborn Children

www.spuc.org.uk

SPUC receives requests from schools and colleges all over the UK, and provides knowledgeable and well-trained speakers to give the SPUC pro-life presentation to students and sixth formers.

SPUC has a team of trained speakers who can visit your school free of charge.

Dr Tom Rogers, SPUC's Education Manager, says: "Every time a SPUC speaker speaks to student   s they are touching the hearts and minds of future generations. That is because they are speaking the truth. A SPUC schools speaker will both change and save lives".

SPUC says: "The school talk is a visual and engaging presentation of our established pro-life position on abortion. It includes video footage of the unborn baby developing in the womb and short interviews with women who speak about their experience of pregnancy and abortion. The 40 minute presentation allows time for a Q&A session and student participation within the usual lesson plan. There is a very positive feedback from teachers and pupils!"

You can contact the Centre for Bio-Ethical Reform. www.cbruk.org

They offer teaching sessions for school years 6 to 7 and 10 to 11.

1) Years 6 to 7: You Are Amazing!

   This is teaching on the value and worth of each human being, from a biological and philosophical perspective. It also addresses relevant topics such as bullying. It is suitable for year group assemblies, PSHE, Religious Studies, Science lessons and youth groups.

2) Year 10 to 11: What Do You Think About Abortion?

This 45 minute session is presented from a scientific and philosophical perspective allowing half the session to be given to class discussion and debate. **What Do You Think About Abortion?** It is suitable for PSHE, Religious Studies, science lessons and youth groups.

For Primary School teachers:

Contact SPUC: www.spuc.org.uk

Support is given to primary school teachers and schools with:

Tiny Feet Club. This provides a fun opportunity for pupils to learn about the beauty of life before birth. The Tiny Feet Club resources are free: (Visit: www.tiny-feet.org)

For University students:

Visit: www.spuc.org.uk

SPUC has student societies, bringing likeminded pro-lifers together to shape and influence their university environment and bring the truth about human life to fellow students at a pivotal time in their lives.

SPUC speaks up for freedom of speech on university campuses. It helps student societies by providing expert speakers, pro-life leaflets and literature, advice on setting up a society and helping with any difficulties which might occur once established. They are keen to keep in touch with students and support them in any way possible.

There is an annual **SPUC weekend Youth Conference** which takes place in March, filled with pro-life talks, workshops and the chance to meet other young pro-lifers. The aim is to bring young pro-life people together, to educate ourselves on the current pro-life issues.

Volunteering:

www.pregnancycrisishelpline.org.uk

There is a need for people to serve in pregnancy crisis centres. If you find that you are not close enough to one to be able to help, you could establish one in your church.

https://lifecharity.org.uk

Options include: Working in a Life charity shop, or becoming a Pregnancy Matters counsellor or skilled listener. You could provide essential administrative support for Life Matters or help out in the office. You could help out in a Life house or distribute baby equipment.

Door-To-Door Leafleting:

SPUC leaflets spread the truth about abortion, euthanasia and other pro-life issues to homes around the UK. Local volunteer members of SPUC distribute leaflets door-to-door. This is the tried and trusted way of reaching large numbers of people with an important message.

Thousands of homes receive SPUC's leaflets on abortion, euthanasia and other current campaigns. More leaders are required to volunteer to co-ordinate local leafleting teams to spread the pro-life message in their area, so that every household has the chance to receive the pro-life message.

Online:

SPUC: Has an active presence on social media. You could be an online advocate. Follow: @SPUCProLife on Facebook, Twitter, Instagram and Youtube.

The Media:

SPUC: Supports people writing to their local and national media. People need to read about why abortion is wrong when they open their newspapers, switch on their TV or tune into their favourite radio programme.

Political Advocacy:

SPUC works to ensure that there is a strong, pro-life voice in Parliament.

For over 50 years SPUC has been at the forefront of the political campaign to give unborn children legal protection. SPUC also campaigns again euthanasia, in particular against the current drive to legalise assisted suicide.

Lobbying MPs is essential to bring about the changes we need to end abortion in this country. For anyone who wants to save women and unborn children from the horror of abortion, SPUC is here to give its members all they need to lobby effectively. SPUC is a grassroots organisation and empowers local people to take effective action.

SPUC monitors the voting records of MPs and MEPs, **working closely with the Westminster government and the devolved governments of Wales, Scotland and Northern Ireland.**

They work to keep people informed about key issues coming before all the UK parliaments. As a first step, we could find out who our MP is and how they rate on pro-life issues.

Contact your MP:

It's your democratic right to lobby your MP on whatever issues matter to you, so let them know you care strongly about protecting life!

As well as your MP, you can also write to other politicians, such as members of the House of Lords and your local councillor.

SPUC is not affiliated to any religious denomination. Many supporters of SPUC are Christian and support SPUC with their prayers as well as taking action locally to spread the pro-life message and change the hearts and minds of local people on abortion.

These are just some examples of how we can get involved practically and begin the process of making abortion a thing of the past.

For I know the plans 'that I have for you'
declares the Lord, '
plans for welfare
and not for calamity
to give you a future and a hope.'

Printed in Great Britain
by Amazon